MITCHAM HISTORIES: 2

NORTH MITCHAM

GW00459230

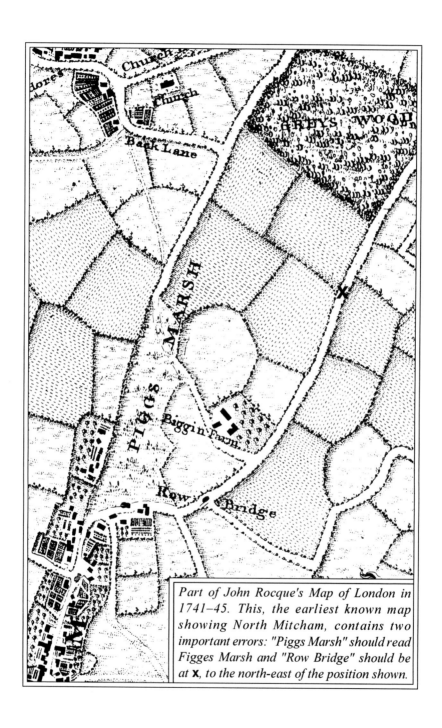

*Part of John Rocque's Map of London in 1741–45. This, the earliest known map showing North Mitcham, contains two important errors: "Piggs Marsh" should read Figges Marsh and "Row Bridge" should be at **x**, to the north-east of the position shown.*

MITCHAM HISTORIES: 2

NORTH MITCHAM

E N MONTAGUE

MERTON HISTORICAL SOCIETY

Published by

MERTON HISTORICAL SOCIETY

2001

© E N Montague 2001

ISBN 1 903899 07 9

Printed by Intype London Ltd

Cover Illustration: Sepia-wash drawing of 'Tamworth Manor House' by J C
Buckler (*c.*1827). This was the residence of James Moore, and to the right and
rear was the farmyard and herbal distillery of the firm of Potter and Moore.
(Original in the possession of the London Borough of Merton)

INTRODUCTION

On the map of the new London Borough of Merton, produced after the reorganisation of London Government in 1965, North Mitcham Ward was shown as an area which comprised mainly early 20th-century housing, shops and light industry. On the south-east it was bounded by what was then British Rail's Southern Region line from Streatham to Mitcham Junction. Commonside East and the A217 London Road lay to the south and west, whilst along its northern border flowed the river Graveney, the ancient boundary between the parishes of Mitcham and Tooting. In extent this was somewhat larger than the North Mitcham Ward known since the days of the Urban District Council in the 1920s, which had ended at Renshaw's Corner and excluded the industrial estates of Streatham Road. Sadly in 1965, merged with much of central Mitcham north and east of the old Fair Green, North Mitcham lost that special political identity which had emerged in the formative years of the Urban District after the end of the 1914–18 War. The process of boundary revision since 1965 has taken this loss of identity further, and for local electoral purposes North Mitcham has disappeared to become Figges Marsh and Graveney Wards. Physically, however, it is still identifiable as the triangle created by the London Road, the Borough boundary to the north, and the railway line to the east. It is this clearly delineated area which shares with Colliers Wood the distinction of being the first part of old Mitcham to become engulfed by the expansion of London in the late 19th century. The history of North Mitcham therefore has a special interest of its own.

A little over a century ago the Graveney was still conspicuous enough as a geographical feature to be used to define the boundary of the new London County Council, a creation of the London Government Act of 1888. Today it is little more than a storm water sewer, largely hidden from public view in a concreted culvert behind terraces of early 20th-century houses. The obvious significance of the river as a line of demarcation has long since vanished, and newcomers to north Mitcham might well be forgiven if they regarded their neighbourhood more as an overspill from Tooting than as a part of the London Borough of Merton. The impression of being remote from the town centre of

Mitcham was even more pronounced in the 1920s, for until Gorringe Park was built over, and the fields of Tamworth Farm were laid out as a public recreation ground and a cemetery, what amounted to a miniature green belt extended eastwards from Colliers Wood almost to the borders of Streatham. Once past Tooting Junction one had the very real impression of leaving the suburbs of pre-1914 London behind, for ahead lay Mitcham, still an attractive village, providing a foretaste of the open Surrey countryside beyond.

Created a political unit by the accidents of historical geography, North Mitcham of necessity rapidly developed a strong identity of its own during the inter-war years. This was soon to find expression through the North Mitcham Improvement Association, one of the most effective pressure groups in the history of the emerging township. Rarely in Mitcham have local government elections engendered such enthusiasm and excitement and, of the many Improvement Association members returned as councillors during the 1920s and '30s, several were to hold office as chairmen of the Urban District Council, or become mayors of the new Borough created in 1934.

Future historians will find material for a definitive history of the political development of North Mitcham in the first three decades of the 20th century in the pages of the local press, council minutes, the magazine of St Barnabas church, and the Improvement Association's own journal, *The North Mitcham Sentinel*. Potentially a fascinating study in itself, this deserves a specialised approach, and might well provide the inspiration for a thesis on local political history. Accordingly it has been treated only superficially in this book, the purpose of which is to bring together for the first time all that is readily available on the earlier history of this part of the London Borough of Merton.

Imperial Measure is used throughout this book. One acre = 0.4047 hectares.

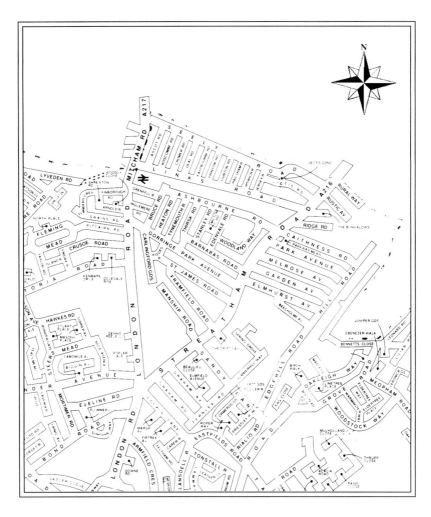

Detail from a modern street map showing the area covered by this book.
Reproduced by permission of Merton Design Unit, London Borough of Merton

ACKNOWLEDGEMENTS

My collection of material for **North Mitcham** commenced some 35 years ago, the quest being greatly facilitated by numerous friends and contacts at Mitcham, Wimbledon, Morden and Wandsworth libraries, archivists at Castle Arch Guildford and in the Minet library of Lambeth and, of course, at the former Surrey Record Office at Kingston. To all of them I will always be grateful, and trust they will understand if I do not mention them by name.

This year (2001), whilst my gleanings were being prepared for publication, numerous drafts were read and re-read with incredible patience by friends and fellow members of Merton Historical Society who form the 'editorial panel' – Judith Goodman, Lionel Green, Tony Scott and lastly, but certainly not least, Peter Hopkins, who also prepared the text and illustrations for the printers. To them I am especially indebted.

Finally, I would like to thank Audrey Thomas who, in addition to reading the text, contacted Patrick Loobey and obtained his consent for photographs of Gorringe Park to be used; and Merton Libraries Department, who many years ago allowed me to copy several old postcards and the drawing of Tamworth House in their possession. These, supplementing various photographs and maps of my own, have been used with good effect by Peter to leaven the text.

E.N.M.

CONTENTS

MAPS AND ILLUSTRATIONS

Chapter 1

THE MIDDLE AGES

The Background

Nothing of archaeological significance has ever been reported from north Mitcham, and there is little to indicate when this part of the parish was first permanently settled. There are, however, signs that before the Norman Conquest, perhaps during the reign of Cnut or his son Harold Harefoot, there may have been people of Scandinavian origin living in the area.

Swains Farm, lying off Swains Lane, could in some way have been connected with Swein, who had a substantial landholding in Tooting during the reign of Edward the Confessor.[1] This idea was suggested by Mawer and Stenton, and although the connection cannot be proved, it is an interesting hypothesis.[2] In its various forms the name Sweyn was not uncommon in England in the 11th century, but the thought that in north Mitcham Swains Farm might embody the memory of a settler of Anglo-Danish descent is certainly intriguing, although it is unlikely ever to be more than conjecture.

The theory of Scandinavian settlement is not without other support, however. The place-name Biggin (as in Biggin Farm) is mentioned in late 13th and early 14th century records dealing with north Mitcham. It is fairly common in the Midlands, where it is derived from the Middle English 'bigging', a building or a house. Further north, and in Scotland, it was more specifically used to mean a roughly-constructed dwelling of clay and wood.[3] Mawer and Stenton considered this place-name element to be of Scandinavian origin. They concluded that since it is of relatively late appearance in Mitcham the name might be attributable to migrants from the Midlands, where it occurs as far south as Hertfordshire which, until the country was united under Athelstan, was on the borders of Danelaw. Tamworth, which as the family name 'de Tamworth'[2] first finds mention in a record of a land holding in north Mitcham in the early 14th century, similarly implies a past link with the Midlands and the area under Danish domination after the 9th century treaty of Wedmore. London, of course, has always attracted merchants and settlement by people of many nationalities. In 1017, following the defeat of Edmund, London with the rest of England actually came under Danish rule. With Merton already a place of note at this time,[4] and connected to London by a major highway, it would not be surprising to find evidence of Danish settlement in the vicinity.

The Domesday survey of 1086 recorded nothing readily identifiable with north Mitcham. A case can be argued, however, for equating this part of the borough with a small estate in Wallington hundred, owned by the abbey of St Peter at Chertsey.[5] Tooting, or more precisely Lower Tooting and Tooting Graveney, on the north bank of the Graveney (and hence in the hundred of Brixton) was also held by Chertsey.[6] At the time of the Conquest the land on the Mitcham side of the border was assessed at a mere half a hide, and therefore quite small – perhaps 60 acres or so in extent. It was in the hands of Wulfward, a Saxon who, we are told, "could turn where he would" – in other words, he was a freeman. By the time of the Domesday survey there was only one tenant family living here, the head of household being classed as a 'cottager' and therefore a person of humble status. The holding included five acres of meadowland, which one would expect to find bordering the river. We can understand how the Domesday clerks failed to describe it as being in Mitcham, for physically, like most of north Mitcham, Wulfward's land was separated from the centre of the village by an area of marshland, a remnant of which still survives as Figges Marsh.

By 1086 Wulfward had been dispossessed, and his land in Wallington hundred, with the rest of Chertsey Abbey's property in Tooting, was in the hands of Hamo, the sheriff of Kent. It seems safe to conclude that Wulfward probably suffered the fate of the majority of the English landowners summoned to the *fyrd* in 1066, and that if he did not actually lose his life, his lands would have been forfeited to the Norman conquerors. Although in value his holding in Mitcham was insignificant, Wulfward had been a man of some substance, for his name appears elsewhere in the Surrey Domesday folios, where he was recorded as owning a further three hides of land in Wandsworth. Here, together with five other freemen in possession of land held directly from King Edward, Wulfward lost his estate to Ansculf (or Ansculf de Picquigny), sheriff of Surrey and Buckinghamshire, one of the great Norman barons.[7]

By the time of the Domesday survey Ansculf was dead, and his estates in Surrey had passed to his son. Some rancour obviously still attached to the manner in which these transfers of title were effected, for the men of Brixton hundred giving evidence to the King's Commissioners conducting the enquiry in 1086 complained that they had "seen neither seal nor a deliverer".

The William Figges, father and son

The earliest record of a grant of land in Mitcham to have come down to us dates from the reign of Henry I, and involved two hides, conveyed to Robert the son of Wolfward *(sic)* and Walter le Poure, to be held *in capite,* i.e. directly of the king.[1] Henry, the third son of the Conqueror, seized the throne of England in 1100 on the death of his brother William II (William 'Rufus', who was shot whilst hunting in the New Forest). Henry had united the Saxon and Norman royal houses by his marriage to Matilda, daughter of Malcolm III of Scotland and niece of Edgar Atheling, and enjoyed a degree of popular support amongst his English subjects for his disapproval of William's rapacious policy. To make his position more secure (his right to the English throne was contested by his eldest brother, Duke Robert of Normandy), and to consolidate dissident factions in the realm, Henry granted a charter promising reform on his accession. Particularly welcomed by the English was his undertaking to abolish oppressive feudal dues, and to reinstate many of the laws of Edward the Confessor.

The idea that the loss suffered by the Saxon Wulfward in the aftermath of 1066 might have been redressed by the return of the land to his son Robert early in the 12th century is attractive, but without documentary support. The grant certainly states that Robert was the son of "Wolfward", but the name (however spelt) was probably not uncommon, and we can by no means be sure it was Robert's father who had been dispossessed after the Conquest. Later records do show a remarkable continuity of tenure of this estate in Mitcham, however, and demonstrate that the heirs of Robert Wolfward (or Fitz Wolfward, as he was sometimes styled) together with le Poure's descendants, retained the trust of the Establishment until the end of the century. Holding the land in 'serjeanty', that is having the duty of performing a specific service to the king, they were government officials, charged with the important responsibility of providing secure accommodation for prisoners arrested by the sheriff in the vill of Mitcham and detained pending appearance before a court. Those apprehended would have been held on suspicion of committing serious crimes, such as homicide, arson, rape, house-breaking and robbery, which lay beyond the jurisdiction of the local moot. Such matters came within the sphere of Henry's justiciar, an office which in the 1120s was held by Ralf Bassett and subsequently his son Richard, both high-ranking judges in what today we would call the office of the Lord Chancellor.

Between 1106 and 1125 the shrievalty of Surrey was held by Gilbert 'the Knight' who, soon after being granted an estate at Merton by King Henry in 1114, had founded the great priory which survived on the banks of the Wandle until 1538. Henry's assignment of the Mitcham land to Fitz Wolfward and le Poure must have preceded his death in 1135, and it could therefore have been either to Gilbert, or later his nephew Fulk, who succeeded him in the office as sheriff from 1126–1129, that Robert and Walter were directly answerable.[2] A document from the reign of John (1199–1216) reiterated the stipulation that detainees, apprehended on the order of the sheriff "either in the fact, or on suspicion of some offence", were to be held for up to "one night and one day" in a house provided "at the owner's proper costs" before being conveyed to the castle at Guildford "with the aid of the County". It was also laid down that Robert Fitz Wolfward and Walter le Poure should provide a 'puntfold', or pound, in which to keep 'distresses', most likely farm stock or domestic chattels seized on the sheriff's orders in lieu of unpaid taxes or fines, or forfeited by convicted felons. In the performance of their duties Fitz Wolfward and Le Poure were required to attend the hundred court at Wallington, and to pay the king by the hand of the sheriff ten shillings a year for the land they held.[3]

During the chaotic reign of Henry III (1216–1272) a Matthew Fitz Bulward contrived to sell part of the estate formerly held by Wolfward and le Poure, and was about to dispose of the remaining portion when, not surprisingly, he was stopped by order of the king. "A writ was directed to the Sheriff, ordering him to see that the king's command herein be obeyed".[4] The land subsequently passed through the hands of various tenants-in-chief, including William le Bule, whose widow Margery was licensed in 1318 to transfer the tenancy to John le Bockyng.[5] The property thus 'alienated' i.e. conveyed, comprised "one messuage, 18 acres of land, 1 acre and a half of meadow and 2s.6d. rent", still held of the king, that is, without any intermediate landlord. Bockyng(e) was described as a "taverner", and is therefore of special interest since he has the distinction of being the first inn-keeper of whom we have record in Mitcham.[6] A similar transfer of tenure occurred in 1332, when Thomas de Sutton received consent to 'enfeoff' the land to Thomas Godard *(sic)*.[7]

Thus it transpired that in the reign of Edward III William Figge appeared on the Mitcham scene, holding as his demesne a "messuage and 16 acres" being, we assume, most of the land originally granted to Wolfward and le Poure.[8] Figge was required to pay five shillings a year in two equal instalments to the sheriff at Easter and Michaelmas, but was otherwise under similar obligations to those of his predecessors two centuries before. He was resident in Mitcham, and an enquiry held in 1326 or 1327, on the death of Hugh le Despenser, junior, confirmed that in addition to his own land "one Fige" had, until a short time before, held a virgate of land (roughly 30 acres) as a tenant of the prior and canons of Merton. The annual rental was four shillings. Precisely where this land lay we are not told, but it is likely to have been in north Mitcham.[9] William Figge would certainly have been a familiar figure at the court at Wallington, for his official duties carried him there every three weeks. He died in 1349, whilst the Black Death was at its height, leaving to his son and heir William the homestead and land in Mitcham, still held directly from the king.[10]

That William Figge the younger remained in Mitcham, where he was undoubtedly regarded as an important member of the community, is evidenced by two entries in the close rolls of Edward III, recording Figge's presence as a witness to the mortgaging in 1357 of the Hall Place estate, owned by Henry de Strete, a London vintner.[11] Figge's name occurs again in 1362, when William Mareys, a major landowner in Mitcham, conveyed a large estate on the banks of the Wandle in trust to the perpetual vicars of Mitcham and 'Westmorden'.[12] William Figge junior died in late 1370 or early 1371, the 44th year of the reign of Edward III, "seized of a house and lands in Mitcham".[13] The name of his immediate successor has not been traced, but Agnes, wife of Geoffrey Prior, who died in 1405/6 during the reign of Henry IV, held a house and land by the same service as the Figges.[14] A family of the Figges' standing, both in the administration of justice and in the parish of Mitcham, would have occupied a house commensurate with their status. As we have seen, what appears to have been the same property, within its 16 or 18 acres of land (accounts vary as to the precise amount), occurs in the records for over 200 years. One could hazard various suggestions as to where the house might have stood but, it must be admitted, these would only be speculation.[15]

If our knowledge of the two William Figges is somewhat sketchy, we are completely ignorant of the names and ultimate fates of their charges. Although it was in disrepair by 1371 and partly demolished in 1379, Guildford Castle was used as a prison throughout the Middle Ages, and in the south-east corner of the 12th-century keep there survives a room, once used as a chapel, on the walls of which can be seen graffiti supposedly carved by prisoners. Had any of these unfortunates been brought before the court at Wallington and, after sentence, afforded such 'hospitality' as the Figges and others cared to procure for them *en route*? By good fortune the Figge family's name has come down to us, but the identities of their charges have, it is sad to say, been lost forever, although some may have achieved a nameless immortality by dint of 'making their mark' on the walls of their cell.

Guildford Castle has long since ceased to be used as a prison, but until 1986 Mitcham remained within the jurisdiction of the South West London Petty Session's Divisional Court at Wallington, and cases arising from offences committed in Mitcham were heard before the magistrates at Wallington.

The Estate of Merton Priory in North Mitcham

From the early 12th century until the Dissolution of the monasteries by Henry VIII north Mitcham fell within one of the many estates belonging to the priory of Merton, in this instance extending beyond the borders of Mitcham into Streatham. Since its foundation shortly before 1117, Merton Priory had attracted many gifts of land, both from major landowning families as well as persons of lesser rank, all motivated by the desire to show favour to the Church, and in the hope of eternal salvation. These benefactions continued throughout the medieval period, with the result that by the close of the 15th century the prior and convent of Merton had become landlords of much of north and north-east Mitcham.

The precise extent of these woods and farmlands is now difficult to establish. It is a reasonable assumption, however, that very broadly they corresponded with the estate over which the prior and convent, as lords of the manor of *'Byggyng 't Tamworth'*, exercised jurisdiction at the time of the Dissolution in 1538, and which survived as the manor of Biggin and Tamworth until the 19th century.[1] If this is correct, the priory's lands would presumably have included the commonland known as Figges Marsh and part of the Upper Green, have extended to the river Graveney and over the border to take in part of Streatham, and as far as Pollards Hill and the parish boundary with Croydon north-east from Mitcham Common.

By whom and when the constituent parts of the priory's lands in Mitcham were granted is not known, but it seems quite possible that the principal benefactor was Henry I's son Robert, the earl of Gloucester, for by the early 14th century the priory's estate in Mitcham was largely held of the honour of Gloucester. It is also feasible that this was, in essence, the holding of the Saxon Brictric who, in the reign of Edward the Confessor, was in possession of land amounting to roughly one fifth of Mitcham and also lying, as far as we can judge, to the north-east and east of the Upper Green. By 1086 much of this estate had been granted by Bishop Odo, one of the Conqueror's half brothers, to the canons of Bayeux. The canons' tenure did not long outlast the bishop's disgrace, however, and by 1088 the property had reverted to the Crown.

At the time of the Domesday survey the remainder of Brictric's lands in Mitcham had been granted by the bishop as two separate holdings of one hide and a half hide (very approximately 120 and 60 acres respectively) to Odbert and Ansgot.[2] Since Odbert possessed land over the border in the vill of Tooting, whilst Ansgot held Streatham, it seems highly likely that their holdings in Mitcham were in the north-east, close to the boundaries of what would eventually emerge as the parishes of Tooting and Streatham.

In 1121 Henry I, son of the Conqueror, assented by charter to the transfer of the royal estate at Merton, including lordship of the manor, to the prior and convent of the newly established priory of Merton. Robert de Caen, Henry's natural son, had been created earl of Gloucester in 1120. He was already a man of great wealth and influence, possessing estates in England totalling many thousands of acres, and it seems, although confirmation is lacking, that as we have already suggested it was Robert who granted the north Mitcham estate to Merton Priory. Earl Robert, who was a staunch supporter of his half-sister the Empress Matilda during the civil war which marked much of Stephen's reign, died in 1147. Whatever befell the Gloucester estates, there appears to have been no adverse impact on the priory's holding in north Mitcham which, as Church property within his diocese, would have enjoyed the protection of the powerful Henry de Blois, bishop of Winchester and brother of Stephen.

What seem to be amongst the earliest recorded tenancies granted in Mitcham by Merton date from the period 1222–31. One of them noted that Giles, the prior, acting in conjunction with the convent, granted to "Roger son of Adam de Mecham and his heirs" half an acre of land called Laca, the rental being one penny per annum. At about the same time "Walter, son of Giles" was granted tenure of a 'messuage', i.e. a house with land and appurtenances, at an annual rental of two shillings. Exactly where these two properties were situated was not specified.[3] Both grants provide examples of the priory using land it had been given as a source of income from rent. In the conditions attached to another tenancy, we have an illustration of how the priory secured labour service as well as an annual income. Some time between 1263 and 1293 a John de Lana was the occupier of a house with four acres of land behind it, owned by the priory. His rent was three shillings, in addition to which he had to provide 24 men for the autumn harvest (the priory supplying them with two meals a day) and 50 men at their "great harvest".[4]

Early in the 13th century Merton Priory had been in possession of land in Mitcham which by ancient custom conferred on the owner or his tenants rights of common pasturage on the parish waste. The precise extent of the lands over which these rights might be exercised was evidently disputed, as can be seen by proceedings in 1240, when the prior of Merton joined with the prior and convent of St Mary at Southwark and other freeholders in Mitcham as plaintiffs in an action against Agnes and William Huscarl of Beddington and others from Beddington and Wallington, alleging that the Huscarls had driven off cattle belonging to the plaintiffs. The court found for the injured parties, who recovered their animals and were awarded 40 shillings damages.[5] In June the same year an assize was held before Stephen de Sequentem and other justices of the king to settle the matter of grazing rights claimed by Mitcham and Beddington, Bandon and Wallington. According to Heales, the evidence of the jury of 12 that the freeholders of Mitcham and the other places had exercised common rights for over 20 years was accepted by the court, and "the damages against prior" were assessed at 40 shillings.[6] The issue was not finally resolved until early in the 19th century, when an inclosure award granted lands formerly part of Mitcham Common, but in Beddington parish, to the Carews of Beddington.[7]

Gifts of land to Merton Priory continued throughout the 13th century. In about 1242, for instance, the prior and convent received from a Richard Duce nine acres of land and a building in Mitcham.[8] Other early gifts were those of "Laurence son of William" who, in 1243, granted to Robert, the prior of Merton, the rental of property in Mitcham worth 20 shillings,[9] and that of Amysius de Wauton or Walton who, in 1248, transferred title of a carucate or hide of land (normally about 120 acres) to the priory.[10]

The Wauton family had held land in Mitcham from the Mauduit family since the early part of the 13th century. Their landlord, Robert Mauduit, one of the great officers of state and chamberlain of the Exchequer from 1194–1222, is said to have purchased properties in Mitcham and South Streatham. Early in the 13th century (possibly during the four years that England lay under the interdict imposed by Pope Innocent III as a punishment for King John's refusal to accept Langton as archbishop of Canterbury) Robert Mauduit received licence from the prior of Southwark for a chapel in his *curia* or "mansion house" at Mitcham.[11] This is an indication that Mauduit and his family were from time to time resident in Mitcham (Robert's duties would, of course, have taken him all over the country) and also suggests that the licence was granted whilst churches in England were closed on papal orders. The licence would therefore have dated to before 1213, when John came to heel and the interdict was lifted. The actual location of the Mauduits' house is unknown, and in 1218 he left Mitcham, granting his property to a William de Teil. It was following the latter's tenancy that tenure passed to the Wautons.

The history of the priory's estate in Mitcham during the remainder of the 13th century is complex and somewhat difficult to follow from the surviving accounts. This is not to say the records are silent, but that it is impossible at this distance in time to correlate satisfactorily the seemingly unconnected events recorded. Thus, in 1230 we have the case of Roger de Walecot and his wife Alice, who sought to establish their right to inherit an estate of 46½ acres, which was contested by the prior of Merton. Henry III directed the sheriff of Surrey to bring the case before the justices at the next assize at Lambeth. The case actually

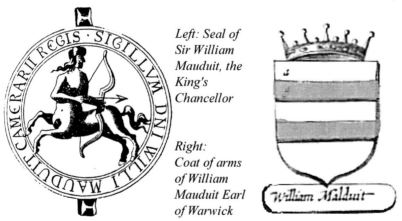

Left: Seal of Sir William Mauduit, the King's Chancellor

Right: Coat of arms of William Mauduit Earl of Warwick

took three years to settle, the "final Concorde" being registered at Westminster in 1233, Roger and Alice being required to surrender the land to William Mauduit on receipt of nine silver marcs.[12] In 1250 the prior and convent of Merton were said to be holding lands in Mitcham of Robert's son, Sir William Mauduit, by the token service of rendering annually a pair of gilt spurs or sixpence.[13] (Sir William, who became the earl of Warwick, followed his father in office, serving as chamberlain of the Exchequer from 1222–1257.) Relations between the priory and Sir William appear not to have been entirely harmonious, for on at least one occasion between 1249 and 1263 it was considered necessary to record formally that Eustace, the prior, and the convent of Merton exonerated Sir William and his heirs from all service due from him as a tenant of land in Mitcham, on payment of agreed sums and the exchange of tokens.[14]

The priory undoubtedly continued in favour with Henry III, however, for while at Merton in 1252 the king confirmed by charter the priory's cherished right of free warren on its Mitcham estate, thus restoring to the prior and convent the freedom to take game and fish on their own land.[15] (This action removed uncertainty which had arisen through the extension of forest law to much of Surrey by the king's grandfather, Henry II.)

In 1291[16] and again in 1314/5 (when the lands and tenements on the estate were valued at £10 per annum) the priory was confirmed to be holding property in Mitcham as a tenant of Gilbert de Clare, earl of Gloucester and Hereford, by the service of providing a quarter of a knight's fee.[17] (The valuation was for taxation purposes, and had as little relevance to its true worth as a modern banding of domestic premises for council tax has to the market value of a house.) For the purposes of the tax imposed by Pope Nicholas IV in 1291 the liability of the priory's estate in Mitcham was assessed at one pound and five shillings.[18] What was presumably the same estate is mentioned in the records in 1347/8, when the country was in the grip of the Black Death. On this occasion it was confirmed at an inquisition *post mortem* following the death of Hugh de Audele, earl of Gloucester, that the priory was holding land described as a quarter of a knight's fee, and valued at merely 30s. per annum.[19]

In 1394 a further valuation of the priory's estate in "the Ville of Michelham", deemed it to have been be worth £14 7s 8d, although this had since been reduced drastically by "a tempest".[20] At the Dissolution the manor of Biggin (whatever this comprised) was recorded as yielding £11 1s 7d in rent.[21]

In 1373, when land owners were still struggling to adapt to the depopulation and consequent decline in the labour force after recurrent outbreaks of plague, Richard Clare was granted leave by letters patent to assign various estates in Mitcham and elsewhere in Surrey to the prior and his successors in perpetuity.[22] A jury called that year to give evidence at an enquiry confirmed that several properties in the parish were already held by the priory. It is frustrating that none of them can be identified with any certainty. Throughout the Middle Ages formal confirmations of the priory's tenure continued to be received and noted in the Merton records, such as that at the inquisition *post mortem* held in 1398/9, following the death of William, brother and heir of Thomas, earl of Stafford, when it was again acknowledged that land at Mitcham, comprising a fourth part of a knight's fee, was held by the prior of Merton.[23]

Biggin Farm which, by the late 19th century, formed an integral part of the north Mitcham estate of Gorringe Park, first received specific mention in 1301, when it was described as "La Bygginge", one of the priory's tenanted properties.[24] A subsidy for his Holy Land campaign had been required by Pope Boniface VIII, and Merton Priory raised the sum required partly from the sale of corn, barley, beans, peas and 'spikings', or lavender, and partly by payments extracted from its various tenants. Biggin, we are told, contributed two shillings. Edward I at this time was in need of finance for his Scottish wars and is said to have prevailed upon the priory to lend him £50 out of the money collected.[25]

Tamworth, which as a place-name in Mitcham is understood to occur in a rental of three crofts of land held in 1531–2 by a William Pratt, was seen by Mawer and Stenton as "probably a manorial name, from the family of John de Tamworth". It is said to be listed amongst the Feet of Fines for 1351 and in the Patent Rolls of 1354, and use of the term 'croft' to describe Pratt's land hints that it originated as enclosures of cleared waste or woodland around a small homestead.[26] In the absence of any other explanation, both Biggin and Tamworth can be assumed to have had their beginnings in separate parts of the priory's Mitcham estate gifted by the earls of Gloucester and Stafford. By the early 16th century the two seem to have merged to form one unit. A clue to the location of the medieval homestead of Biggin may exist in the position of Tamworth House, a newly-built 'Regency' villa shown on early 19th century plans to have occupied a site between Biggin Farm and Streatham Lane.

Following the Dissolution, much of the priory's Mitcham estate, together with lordship of the manor of "Bygging" and Tamworth, was granted by Henry VIII in 1544 to Robert Wilford, a London merchant,[27] who was already in possession of an estate in Lower Mitcham inherited from his father James Wilford.[28] The priory's lands had extended into Tooting Graveney, Streatham and Clapham, and comprised 640 acres, including 200 of woodland.[29] "Estmicham" and the "Mareshlandes" in Mitcham and Carshalton are mentioned in the Ministers' Accounts of 1538.[30] In north Mitcham Wilford's holding took in Biggin Farm, part of "Fenny Mead" (later known as Fleming Mead),[31] and extended to the "Amery Lands" and "Begrave Hill", both in the Colliers Wood area.

The coat of arms of the present London Borough of Merton incorporates the fret from Merton Priory's arms as well as three sprigs of Mitcham lavender.

LOT 81
THE VALUABLE AND EXTENSIVE

MANOR OF BIGGIN & TAMWORTH,

With Court Baron, Court Leet, Quit Rents, Fines Arbitrary, Heriots, Royalties, Tolls, Rights Members, Privileges, and Appurtenances, extending over all Parts of the Commons and Wastes in the Parish of Mitcham, of about

565 ACRES.

	£	s.	d.
The Copyhold Tenants of this Manor are 65 in number, and pay annual Quit Rents, amounting to about	11	5	0
The fines upon admission have realised annually upon an average of the last ten years	150	0	0
The Tolls of the Fair on Mitcham Green have realised annually upon an average of the last ten years (subject to trifling costs of collection)	19	13	10
The sale of Gravel, &c., from the Commons, has realised upon an average of the last five years (net)	24	0	0
Total per annum	£204	18	10

A Common Keeper has been appointed by the respective Lords claiming rights over the Commons, and a Lease has been granted to such Common Keeper, a copy of which will be produced at the sale.

The customs of the Manor are, as to the descent of Copyholds, of the nature of Borough English, the Estates descending to the youngest son. The Lord is entitled, for a Heriot on the death of every Copyholder, to the best animal but in a few instances to a given sum as a Heriot certain. The fine is arbitrary upon admission, on death, or alienation, except in a few instances where the fine is certain. The arbitrary fines have been generally assessed upon two years' improved annual value of the Copyhold.

The Manor is offered with such rights as the Lord may, as such, be entitled to in and over the soil of the extensive and valuable Commons and Waste Lands in the parish of Mitcham, and subject to such Rights of Common as the tenants of the Manor and others may be entitled to, and subject also to an annual Farm-rent of £1 5s. 7d., reserved by the Grant of the Manor by Henry the Eighth, and now payable to John Routh, Esq.

The rare advantages of possessing such a property as this to professional gentlemen and others, particularly so near the Metropolis, with the extensive Commons and Wastes in the parish (which, no doubt, will, at no far distant period, be inclosed, and thereby rendered even more valuable and desirable in many respects), together with the powers and benefits given to Lords of Manors by the Copyhold Enfranchisement Acts, are so well known as not to require further comment or recommendation.

GARRAWAY'S COFFEE HOUSE, 'CHANGE ALLEY, CORNHILL, LONDON.
August, 1853.

Sale Particulars, Manor of Biggin and Tamworth 1853.

THE MANOR OF BIGGIN AND TAMWORTH

Although the point at which the manor of Biggin and Tamworth came into being remains somewhat obscure, Brayley (not, it must be said, always a totally reliable authority) was prepared to speculate that it was "probably one of the manors held by Fitz-Ansculf at the time of the Domesday survey".[1] The word 'manor' did not come into use in England until after the Conquest, and it was not actually used by the Norman clerks to describe either of Fitz-Ansculf's holdings in Mitcham. Like many of his contemporaries, Brayley was using the term to convey the common conception of a manor as a unit of local administration, coterminous with but distinct from the ecclesiastical parish, dominated by the squire and ruled through the courts baron and leet. In reality the situation in medieval England was often very different and more complex. Brayley quoted no evidence in support of his supposition, and his comment is best ignored.

We have examined in the previous chapter the evidence showing that, by the mid-13th century, Merton Priory was in possession of a large estate in Mitcham. Without doubt this incorporated one or more former Saxon holdings, and we can be sure that to the customs and practices followed since before the Conquest new procedures would have been introduced by the prior and convent for the control of their tenantry and the efficient running of the property. The manor of Biggin emerged during the 12th century as an area in which the priory also administered criminal justice, the annals of Merton recording that it was proved to the satisfaction of the king's justices sitting at Guildford in 1278 that the 'liberties' or privileges enjoyed by the priory in its estates in various parts of Surrey had been granted by Henry II in the latter half of the 12th century. These included not only the right of *sac* and *soc* (to hold and control a manorial court and receive profits and services), but also *thol* and *theam* (to try and punish offenders), and *infangenetheof* and *outfangenetheof* (the right to arrest and sentence thieves and, if necessary, to pursue them should they flee the manor).[2]

These were difficult times, and the severity with which the prior and convent were prepared to deal with miscreants can be judged by the report to the Bermondsey assize in 1258 that the prior had erected a gallows at Merton.[3] Precisely where this was is not stated, but the evidence suggests it could well have been on a small patch of common land near where Church and Western Roads now meet Christchurch Road, just outside the priory precinct. Here, at a cross roads where the parishes of Merton and Mitcham met, was a typical site where the consequences of wrong-doing could be made plain to all who passed by. Known locally as Jacob's Green, a small piece of waste land survived here until the early 20th century. The court rolls confirm that it was regarded as being waste within the manor of Biggin and Tamworth, and record several grants of enclosure during the 19th century by which it was progressively reduced in extent.[4] Whether or not the priory's gibbet was a permanent feature here during the Middle Ages is not known, but the memory of it seems to have been enshrined in the names by which nearby fields like Hanging Hook, Hanging Field and Hell's Acre, were still known as late as the 1840s.[5]

In 1314/15 the prior and convent of Merton were confirmed to be holding the manor of Biggin, comprising lands and tenements at Mitcham worth £10 p.a., as tenants of Gilbert de Clare, earl of Gloucester,[6] and the last four priors before the Dissolution are recorded in the court rolls as lords of the manor of Biggin in "Mycham" in 1484, 1502, 1520 and 1537.[7] As the manor of Biggin and Tamworth, by which name it was known after passing into lay ownership, the estate is not mentioned until 1538, when the *Firma Man' de Byggyng 't Tamworth* appears in the ministers' accounts listing property belonging to Merton Priory.[8] The perquisites of the manor court at Mitcham, i.e. fines, quit rents etc., were then valued at 7 shillings a year.[9] In 1544 lordship of the manor, together with an estate comprising land in Carshalton, Tooting Graveney and Streatham as well as Mitcham, was granted to Robert Wilford (or Wylforde), "Citizen and Merchant Taylor of London", and his wife Joan.[10]

The rolls of the manor covering the years from 1484 to 1882 survive, and are in the care of Surrey History Centre. The earlier rolls, unfortunately for many students today, still await translation from the Latin in which they continued to be written by the stewards' clerks until the 17th century. Together with nine rentals and terriers of 1861, and plans of various properties still within the jurisdiction of the manor in the 19th century, the collection is a readily accessible and potentially important source of local history material for future research.

Through the medium of these records and published histories the descent of the lordship of "Bigging in Mitcham", and subsequently of the manor of Biggin and Tamworth, can be traced with ease. It was the general practice of topographical and county historians writing in the late 18th and 19th centuries to recount in great detail the passage of ownership of the manors, for the subject was one of considerable interest and fascination to their wealthy patrons and others who, it was anticipated, would purchase the published works. Thus Daniel Lysons, supplied with extracts from the court rolls of Biggin and Tamworth by Richard Barnes, the steward of the manor, gave the following summary in 1792:–

> "The manor Bigging and Tamworth belonged to Merton Abbey, and was granted by Henry VIII after the suppression of that monastery to Robert Wilford, merchant taylor, for the sum of £486 14s. In 1569 it appears to have been the property of John Lord Mordaunt, in right of his wife. In 1582 Henry Whitney, Esq., held a court as lord of this manor, though it appears that he purchased a moiety thereof the ensuing year of Robert Aprece, Esq. The Whitneys alienated the manor in 1603 to Sir John Carrill. Three years afterwards it belonged to John Lord Hunsdon, whose son sold it in 1614 to Sir Nicholas Carew, alias Throckmorton. It was alienated about the year 1655 to Edward Thurland, Esq., and continued in the same family till 1744, when it was purchased of the devisees of another Edward Thurland by John Manship, Esq., father of the present proprietor." [11]

Wilford obviously had the financial resources to meet the king's price, and by his purchase of the lordship of the manor, together with a large estate, greatly enhanced his social status. Unfortunately Robert Wilford had not long to enjoy his newly acquired position in local society, for he died in September 1545. His will was proved at London two months later. [12] In it he left to his wife "Johane"

> "All that manner of Biggin with appurtenances in Mitcham and all the capital messuage or tenement with appurtenances and all my other messuages, lands and tenements in Mitcham and elsewhere in

the county of Surrey to have and to howld for life, and after her death to William Wilford my son and heir apparent. In default of issue, to Anne Wilford, Johan Wilford and Auderey Wilford my daughters. In default of issue, to Nicholas Wilford my brother."

Following Robert Wilford's death Joan remarried, taking as her second husband Lord Mordaunt. It was in part through the Wilfords' daughter Anne, who married a Henry Whitney, "servant to Sir Thomas Bromley, the Lord Chancellor", that the lordship of the manor of Biggin and Tamworth passed into the hands of the Whitney family. The portion purchased from Aprece, or "Apprice", had been the inheritance of Anne's sister and co-heir Johan, whom Robert Aprece had married. In July 1580, at Henry Whitney's request, Queen Elizabeth confirmed the grant of free warren in his domain lands in Mitcham, originally granted by Henry III to Merton Priory.[13] The important right to hunt was thus secured for the Whitneys and future owners of the manor, and this remained a valued manorial asset until the closing years of the 19th century, when the taking of game in the woodlands towards Pollards Hill was the preserve of those possessing the shooting rights.

The Whitneys retained lordship of the manor of Biggin and Tamworth until the reign of James I and then, in June 1603, they sold it, together with various parcels of land in Mitcham totalling 100 acres, plus land and appurtenances in Tooting Graveney and Streatham, to Sir John Carryll *(sic)* of Warnham, Sussex.[14] Sir John in his turn sold to the Rt. Hon. Sir John Carey from whom the manor was purchased by Carew in 1614.[15] As can be seen from Lyson's account above, several further changes of ownership ensued during the reign of James I.

The Carews, whose seat was at Beddington, were Royalists and suffered as a consequence of their support of Charles I during the Civil War. Sir Nicholas died in 1644, and was succeeded by his eldest son, Sir Francis, usually described as "of Reigate". Sir Francis, his finances in ruins and heavily penalised by Parliament for his loyalty to the Crown, was obliged to mortgage his Norbury and Mitcham estates in 1647. He died in 1649, still in debt, and lordship of the manor of Biggin and Tamworth passed from his widow Mary into the hands of Edward Thurland of Reigate and the Inner Temple.[16] Thurland, "a gentleman entitled to bear arms", amongst other positions held the stewardship of the estate of the earl of Warwick. He was also a senior justice of the peace, often taking the chair at Surrey quarter sessions. His sphere of activity on the bench appears to have been mainly in the Reigate area, where he was a prominent citizen.[17] John Manship, to whom Thurland's son Edward sold the manor in January 1744/5, was a director of the East India Company, already resident in Mitcham at The Canons, which he had leased a few years previously from the Cranmer family. Having acquired a substantial estate in Mitcham, as well as the lordship of the manor of Biggin and Tamworth, Manship most likely intended moving with his family and household to Biggin Grove, possibly after rebuilding or refurbishment, but this was not to be and he died in 1749 whilst still resident at The Canons.[18]

Manning and Bray set out the descent of the manor in considerably more detail than outlined above, and further elaboration here is unnecessary.[19] Manship devised the estate to his wife Elizabeth during her lifetime, after which it passed to his only son, John. In 1804 the latter sold the manor and the family estate in Mitcham to James Moore, proprietor of the firm of Potter and Moore, physic gardeners and distillers of essential oils, who thereupon became a major landowner in Mitcham.

Until more work is possible on the surviving documents, the actual extent of the land within the manor's jurisdiction must remain somewhat uncertain. *The Victoria County History of Surrey,* unfortunately wrong in so many details in its account of Mitcham, is only partly correct in asserting that the manor lay "beyond the railway bridge off the Croydon Road".[20] Several houses in central Mitcham are known to have been copyhold of the manor, including Durham House and the Nag's Head public house, both of which overlooked Upper Green West, as well as land in north Mitcham.[4] In 1544, when the manor extended beyond the bounds of Mitcham into the neighbouring parishes of Tooting Graveney and Streatham, it comprised 640 acres, including 200 acres of wood, and much of the common pasture or waste land of Mitcham.[21] As late as the mid-19th century it included, in the extreme north-west of the parish, several small parcels of common land. As we have seen, one of these, Jacob's Green, abutted surviving fragments of the precinct wall of Merton Priory,[4] whilst others lay either side of the river Wandle at Phipps Bridge.[22] These plots of waste ground were obviously vestiges of the former priory estate and had passed with the manor to Robert Wilford in 1544.

In the late 18th century it was to the lady of the manor of Biggin and Tamworth that the parish officers applied for consent to enclose part of Mitcham Common for the erection of a new workhouse, and 30 years later permission was given by James Moore for a further enclosure of common land to provide a site for a windmill. The Upper, or Fair, Green was by custom the venue for the annual Mitcham Fair, tolls from which were collected from the showmen by the steward of the manor, and the then 50 or so acres of Figs, Figges or 'Pigges' Marsh comprised another portion of the parish waste acknowledged to be within the manor.[23]

It is evident from a series of enclosure grants made in the mid-19th century that the lord of the manor still claimed, and was exercising without apparent opposition or protest, rights over areas of roadside waste remaining in several parts of Mitcham. Including those mentioned above, land fronting London Road north of the Swan inn as far as Tooting parish boundary, and other plots bordering Mitcham Common along Commonside East up to New Barns Farm were fenced off and sold.[4]

When rights over the main expanse of Mitcham Common were in dispute between 1801 and 1819 and wholesale enclosure was proposed, it was claimed for the lord of the manor of Biggin and Tamworth that his jurisdiction extended over the entire Common lying within the civil and ecclesiastical parish of Mitcham. This was, however, strongly contested by the lords of the other Mitcham manors of Mitcham Canons, Ravensbury and Vauxhall, and also by the lord of the manor of Beddington and Bandon. It required lengthy litigation, culminating in a High Court ruling delivered on appeal, before the boundaries of Biggin and Tamworth on Mitcham Common, and those of the other manors, were settled.[24]

In James Moore's time a Common keeper and herdsman was appointed jointly by the lords of the Mitcham manors to prevent over-grazing and to impose a measure of control over the exercise of other common rights, such as the gathering of wood and turves for fuel. By the end of the century, when very few copyholders were left and rights to common pasture were rarely exercised, it was no longer felt necessary to safeguard the interests of the remaining tenants of the manor, and James Bridger, Moore's successor, seldom, if ever, took steps to curb unauthorised grazing.[25]

In August 1853, two years after Moore's death and on the instructions of the executors, the "Valuable and extensive Manor of Biggin and Tamworth" was offered for sale by public auction. The value of the manor, both as a source of rents and income from the fines and levies arising from the proceedings of its courts and, perhaps more importantly, as a source of profit from the enclosure and sale of common land for building purposes, was stressed in the particulars prepared for the enticement of likely buyers. Annual quit rents from copyhold tenants amounted to £11 5s 0d, and fines or fees levied upon admissions to tenancy of the manor had averaged £150 over the previous ten years. With fair tolls and the sale of gravel from the Common the total income was a little over £200 p.a.[26]

Following the auction lordship of the manor passed to James Bridger, Moore's natural son, who also secured possession of the family business and much of his late father's freehold land and buildings. Within four years of Moore's death grants of enclosure of what in total amounted to a substantial area of common 'waste' lying within the manor, were made to owners of the adjacent land. In the main these enclosures involved parcels of land bordering Figges Marsh, Commonside East and Phipps Bridge Road, and the majority were formalised at a general court baron and customary court of the manor in January 1858. Although at first sight it might appear that Bridger was indulging in what today would be considered 'asset stripping', there may well have been a need to raise money to meet the many and generous bequests made by Moore in his will. A shortage of working capital after the estate had been settled could also have presented problems. Whatever the immediate reasons, piecemeal disposal of the former Moore estate continued over the next 30 years, and by the early years of the 20th century, the compilers of the *Victoria County History* could comment that "Almost all the manor of Tamworth has been parcelled out as a building estate."

Bridger died in 1885, and lordship of the manor was sold in 1888,[27] passing through the hands of Paine and Brettell, solicitors of Chertsey, before being acquired by the Prince's Golf Club which had negotiated a lease of part of Mitcham Common from the newly created Board of Conservators.[28] For several years there had been growing concern, expressed both locally and nationally, at the exercise by Bridger and other lords of the Mitcham manors of their rights to remove unlimited quantities of turf and gravel from the Common. Threatened legal action by those anxious to secure preservation of what was becoming appreciated as valuable open space for public enjoyment culminated in the vesting of the mineral rights in the Conservators in 1894. The diminution of the powers and profitability of the manor of Biggin and Tamworth continued with the acquisition in 1905 of the franchise of the annual Mitcham Fair by the Board of Conservators, who saw a need to control the fair more effectively to reduce nuisance and inconvenience to the general public. With the exception of the central core of Figges Marsh and the Fair Green, common lands formerly within the undisputed control of the manor had been parcelled out as building estates during Bridger's tenure, and most of the copyholds had been enfranchised. On the general extinction of manorial rights in the 1920s lordship of the manor became defunct.

General view of Figges Marsh from the south, showing a row of tall trees following the old hedge line between the Marsh and former enclosures of Biggin Farm (1970)

FIGGES MARSH

Figges Marsh, a fragment of the once extensive common 'waste' or
rough pasture surrounding the medieval village of Mitcham, survives
today as some 26 acres of virtually featureless greensward forming a
triangle of open space between Streatham Road and London Road.
Beneath its eastern margin flows one of Mitcham's forgotten
watercourses, the Little Graveney or, as it is known by the drainage
engineers, the "Main Ditch". This rises at the foot of Pollards Hill, and
flows in a generally north-westerly direction to join the river Graveney
in the vicinity of Tooting station, but is now confined underground in a
culvert and hidden from view.[1] Early in the 20th century the Little
Graveney was very much in evidence as a substantial rivulet at the side
of Figges Marsh, and until disease necessitated their felling early in
1973 its course was still marked by a line of massive elms which had
probably started their lives as hedgerow saplings.[2] Now the course of
the culvert can be traced by a series of manhole covers in the tarmac
path running north-west across Figges Marsh from the Streatham Road.
Parallel to it, a slight depression can just be detected in the grass, caused
by settlement of the spoil used to fill the redundant ditch.[3] Out of sight
the watercourse may be, but it is still capable of making its presence
known somewhat dramatically, one memorable occasion being during
the summer of 1973 when, after a sudden storm, the Little Graveney
overflowed and brought traffic on the Streatham Road to a standstill.[4]

Under the thin topsoil of Figges Marsh is a stratum of river terrace
gravel overlying the London Clay which forms the gently rising ground
to the north-east. The irregular outline of a pond, probably an old gravel
pit, can be seen at the northern apex of the Marsh on the 25-inch O.S.
map of 1867. Evidently short-lived, it had been back-filled and levelled
by 1891. As one might expect, the water table is never far from the
surface here, and after a spell of prolonged wet weather it is still not
unknown for this corner of the Marsh, near where Gorringe Park Avenue
meets the London Road, to be boggy, if not actually under a sheet of
water. In 1970 one of the last of Mitcham's surface air raid shelters
was removed from this spot, and for some years afterwards it was
apparent that consolidation of the subsoil had impeded the flow of

ground water. Suggestions were made at the time that if the nuisance from standing water persisted the parks department should admit defeat, recreate the pond and landscape the surrounding ground.[5]

The high water table beneath much of Figges Marsh is the most likely reason for its being left uncultivated, although parts were pressed into service as allotment gardens in both World Wars. It is not difficult to understand how the Marsh survived as unenclosed waste whilst other, potentially more productive land, remained to be cleared and brought under cultivation. To the west of the London Road the topsoil becomes deeper, and it would seem probable that by the Middle Ages the land here had been brought under the plough as an extension of the open West Field of the village, or was enclosed as farmland.[6] On the other side of the Marsh, where the land rises very slightly and is thus better drained, fragments of the original woodland cover may have survived until the expansion of farming in the 16th century. Greys Woods, over the Streatham boundary, remained until the early 19th century,[7] and when, soon after the end of the Napoleonic Wars, Biggin Farm and the adjacent Tamworth House (later to become Gorringe Park) were offered for sale the auctioneers could still draw prospective purchasers' attention to the estate's wealth of "fine-grown trees".[8] In the 1860s the land now covered by the houses of Inglemere and Grenfell Roads was shown on contemporary maps as a corner of woodland, most likely a secondary growth of mixed deciduous trees with an undergrowth of wetland species.

The earliest known documentary reference to "Figgesmarsh" occurs in a collection of deeds spanning the period 1606–1699, now in the Surrey History Centre.[9] Use of the term 'marsh' was obviously appropriate and, as we have seen in an earlier chapter, Figge was the name of a local family holding land in the 14th century. Although Figges Marsh remained the name used for official purposes, during the late 18th and early 19th centuries 'Pig's Marsh' was adopted by several map makers.[10] This seems to have arisen from a topographer's error, being first used by John Rocque in his map of the environs of London in 1741–5. His maps unfortunately do contain a number of mistakes, but 'Pig's Marsh' could have been in common use at the time, prompted by the land's swampy nature and its use by swine herds.

Most interestingly, Rocque shows no road on the western side of Figges Marsh, the route from Mitcham to Tooting in the early 1740s (if we assume his omission of the present London Road was not an oversight) being from Streatham Lane by a lane leading past Biggin (Rocque called it "Bagen") Farm. This detour to the east may well have been brought about by the need to avoid the marsh. His map of Surrey, published some 20 years later, shows that by the 1760s the present straight section of the London Road north from the Swan was in existence, presumably having been constructed a few years previously by the turnpike trust. The old road to Tooting survived as a winding lane through the grounds of Gorringe Park until the early 20th century, and was eventually replaced by the first part of St James Road and then Gorringe Park Avenue.

The name 'Pig's Marsh' would certainly have sounded unattractive to many new residents in the early Victorian period, and it is interesting to see a desire to improve the image of one property reflected in the Post Office *Directory* for 1862, where the address of Albert Grover's Poplars Academy – a prestigious boarding school – is given as "Tamworth Green". This did not influence the surveyors of the Ordnance Survey however, and in the first edition of the 25-inch map in 1867 Figges Marsh was the name accepted as correct by the official map-makers.

The ancient custom of turning out livestock to graze on the Marsh or, indeed, on other common lands in the parish, was jealously guarded by those (usually copyholders of one or other of the four Mitcham manors) who claimed the right. Whereas control of the use of 'commonable' lands had often become vested in the lordships of the manors in which they lay, it was not unknown in Mitcham, and no doubt elsewhere, for the vestry to intervene in the interests of the parish as a whole. Thus in October 1801, during a period in the Napoleonic War when nationally the steeply rising cost of wheat boosted the profits to be derived from arable farming, and brought about a reduction in the area of pasture, Mitcham vestry resolved that Figges Marsh should be surrounded by "ditches, gates and fences" the better to control grazing.[11] In Mitcham the need to safeguard the rights of commoners was made more urgent because 240 acres of arable and permanent pasture, equal to one tenth of the parish, were converted to 'garden grounds' for the growing of medicinal or aromatic herbs, and therefore lost to food production, in the six years from 1796 to 1802. The vestry's resolution was evidently acted upon, and the remains of the ditches and hedges can be seen around much of the Marsh in the six inch to the mile O.S. map of 1865.

In 1804 lordship of the manor of Biggin and Tamworth was purchased by James Moore. This was at the height of the agrarian revolution, when large tracts of common land were being enclosed in pursuit of greater farming efficiency. Two years later, surveyor John Middleton (engaged by the dean and chapter of Canterbury to report on the potential for enclosing waste within the manor of Vauxhall, which included part of Mitcham) observed that "Piggs Marsh, which contains about 50 acres, is supposed to be in the manor of Biggin".[12] For long a dominant personality in Mitcham, Moore seems in general to have respected commoners' rights, although instances can be cited of enclosure of marginal land within the manor being sanctioned during his lifetime. Following his death in 1851 the pace of change quickened, but very little of Mitcham Common itself was affected, mainly because of uncertainty as to the extent of the individual manors' jurisdiction, but also growing opposition to the loss of open space for public enjoyment.

In north Mitcham there was evidently no such uncertainty. The tithe map of 1847 shows that a large field, described in the accompanying register as a "New Inclosure", had been created since the sale of the adjoining Biggin Farm in 1822 and added to the farm. This happened whilst James Moore was alive, and the process was to continue under his son. Between January and June 1855 enclosure of a long strip of roadside waste, extending roughly from where Arnold Road now joins the London Road southwards to Eveline Road, was formally sanctioned by the manor court of Biggin and Tamworth.[13] In each case the waste, some of it already enclosed, went to the owners of adjacent property, the largest portion being added to land in the possession of the Revd Humphrey Waldo-Sibthorpe, whose family had been major landowners in Upper Mitcham since the 18th century. The manorial court in 1855 also agreed to the enclosure of roadside land opposite the Swan Inn, and it would seem that during the 30 years that Bridger was lord of the manor the acreage of common waste, of which Figges Marsh itself formed a major part, was effectively halved. The land enclosed was usually lost to the commoners forever and, of course, added considerably to the value of the plots with which it was amalgamated.

Use of the Marsh as grazing land lasted for a few more years, with the occupiers of Swains Farm exercising rights of common pasture until well into Victoria's reign. The last of these seems to have been John Henry Bunce who, as a tenant of James Moore and later of James Bridger in the 1850s and '60s, rented the farmstead in Swains Lane with its house, a cottage, stable, barn, piggeries and dairy.[14] Bunce was primarily a market gardener, but he kept a dozen cows in milk. Since he lacked sufficient grassland of his own, he turned his cattle out to graze on Figges Marsh under the care of boys to ensure the animals were kept from straying onto the surrounding enclosures. James Weston of Pound Farm, Upper Mitcham, a contemporary of Bunce who farmed land in the East Field, turned out a similar number of cattle on the southern part of the Marsh.[15]

By 1890 public protest at the manner in which Mitcham Common was being destroyed by gravel digging or threatened with enclosure for private gain led to the successful passage through Parliament of the Metropolitan Commons (Mitcham) Supplemental Bill the following year. Under the Act management of the common lands of Mitcham was placed in the hands of a Board of Conservators, and Figges Marsh, together with the other Mitcham greens, passed into their guardianship. This remained the situation for the next quarter century. During World War I Mitcham acquired the status of an Urban District, and civic pride soon dictated that the Council should take control of the public open spaces within the town centre. A private Act, the Mitcham Urban District Council Act of 1923, having granted the necessary authority, in 1924 responsibility for Figges Marsh, together with the Upper and Lower Greens, the Cricket Green, Cranmer Green and the Three Kings Piece was transferred to the Council.

Apart from the land used temporarily as allotment gardens during the 1914–18 war, Figges Marsh remained briefly much as it had always been, an area of rough common which, with old parkland and fields on either side, separated Mitcham from the expanding suburbs of London.

The Figges Marsh of the inter-war years can still be recalled by older residents of Mitcham. Those who were children in the late 1920s and early 1930s can probably remember the tents and animals of a little travelling circus that appeared annually at the northern tip of the Marsh; they may also recall the caravans and horses of the gypsies who would camp amongst the gorse bushes until moved on by the local authority.

Forty years later, a regime of regular gang-mowing by the Council's parks department had resulted in Figges Marsh losing completely any resemblance it may once have had to a rough Surrey common, and its former diversity of heathland flora was effectively suppressed. Second World-War allotment gardens near Streatham Road had been removed by the 1950s. Sports pitches next covered the Marsh, the main use of which during the week was for the 'exercising' of local dogs, much to the disgust of the footballers. Flat as the proverbial pancake, by the 1960s Figges Marsh was the soulless epitome of a municipal common, surrounded by well-disciplined and characterless trees.

Apart from the ending of football on the Marsh, little has changed in the intervening 40 years, and today Figges Marsh offers nothing to catch the eye apart from a welcome patch of green in the otherwise unbroken expanse of bricks and mortar which is our legacy from the 1920s and '30s.

Figges Marsh (looking north) 1975

TOOTING JUNCTION TO LAVENDER AVENUE

Road and Rail

Strictly speaking, old Tooting railway station was situated just outside the boundary of the ancient ecclesiastical parish of Mitcham, later to become the Borough of Mitcham. Nevertheless, the station was to play an important role in the development of the town's northern fringes towards the close of the 19th century by facilitating commuter mobility to and from the expanding suburbs of South London. The effect can be seen in the Ordnance Survey map of 1894–96. The Gorringe Park Hotel, an imposing public house at the end of the terrace of shops in London Road close by the station, was leased by Young & Co. in 1892, and bought in 1898. The pace increased as the century drew to a close, and by the time the map was revised in 1911 rows of houses and shops had been built either side of the road to Mitcham as far as Figges Marsh.

Now a private residence, the original station lies off the main road to London, in Longley Road. Although what remains of its former platform is fenced off from the railway line, and the fields that originally surrounded it have long since disappeared beneath the bricks and mortar of Greater London, the little building still retains much of the appearance of a small country station. It was built for the Tooting, Merton and Wimbledon Joint Railway Company, authorised by Act of Parliament

Tooting Station (disused) c.1975

in 1864, but a year later, by a further Act, land acquired by the local company was vested in the larger London Brighton and South Coast Railway. The official opening of Tooting station, on behalf of the consortium, took place on 1 October 1868.

The development of Tooting and North Mitcham in the succeeding decades was soon to render a more commodious and better placed station necessary to meet the needs of the steadily increasing traffic, and in August 1894 Tooting Junction station was opened on the bridge carrying the London Road across the tracks of the London & South Western and the London Brighton and South Coast Railways connecting Streatham with Wimbledon. The pendulum of fortune was soon to swing the other way, however, for competition from the new electric tramways, extended to Mitcham by 1906, was to have a serious impact on the profitability of the suburban railways. The branch line from Tooting Junction to Wimbledon via Merton Park was finally shut down to passenger traffic in March 1929, many years after it had ceased to be a viable element in the Southern Railway Company's operations. Five years later the junction at Tooting was severed, but it was not until much later that 'Junction' was dropped from the official title of the 'new' station on the bridge, and the more accurate 'Tooting Station' adopted.

Served from Wimbledon, the 'Merton Abbey Loop' remained in use for goods only until May 1972, and the track was finally removed shortly afterwards. The new housing estates of Flanders Crescent and Singlegate Close were built on land released by the old line and its sidings in the 1980s, and during the development the redundant footbridge linking Robinson Road and Swains Road was removed. The bridge over the track from Tooting to Haydons Road remains, providing pedestrian access between Lyveden and Longley Roads.

Since long before the railways, southbound travellers had entered Mitcham over Tooting bridge, which crossed the Graveney as it flowed from Norbury to join the Wandle at Colliers Wood.[1] Until the later years of the 19th century the river remained a visible landmark conveniently delineating much of the boundary between the two civil parishes, but the Graveney has now to a large extent joined the ranks of London's forgotten watercourses, and in the vicinity of Tooting station it has been banished underground. The parapet of the old bridge was visible for many years between Nos. 2 and 2a Seeley Road but has now been obscured. The river itself emerges from its culvert below the Longley Road footbridge, and can be seen flowing westwards behind the back fences of houses in Lyveden Road, running parallel to the railway line. Sadly, the days are gone when, in its deeper stretches, small boys could fish for minnows, or work off animal high spirits becoming gloriously wet and muddy at no risk to themselves and with little annoyance to the public at large.

On the western side of the London Road, opposite Figges Marsh and near the point where Victoria Road joins the main road, there stands a milestone, much eroded by the elements and with its inscriptions 'Whitehall 7½' and 'Royal Exchange 8' now indecipherable. One of a series, a few of which can still be found, this was erected in compliance with the Turnpike Acts of George II by the Trustees of the Surrey and Sussex Roads who, from 1755 until the middle of the next century, were responsible for the construction and maintenance of the highway from Kennington Common through Tooting and Mitcham to Sutton.[2]

As we have observed in the previous chapter, it appears from the evidence of Rocque's maps that it was the turnpike trust that was responsible, probably in the late 1750s, for constructing today's straight section of the London Road between Gorringe Park Avenue and the Swan. Before then the way to Mitcham had been by a winding lane which skirted the eastern side of the Marsh, passing Biggin Farm to meet the lane from Streatham.

The milestone at Figges Marsh c.1970

Until 1 November 1865 the Trust's Figges Marsh tollgate barred the
road near where it is now joined by Inglemere Road.[3] Here, on the
eastern, or Marsh side of the road, there was a deep ditch formed by the
Graveney, whilst the small tollhouse with a length of fence stood on
the opposite side, where there was also a pond. In very wet weather
both ditch and pond overflowed and flooded the road. Pedestrians were
obliged to cross by a little wooden footbridge, unless the flooding was
too extensive, when a cart was employed to ferry them to and fro.[4] The
gate had been positioned with the intention of making it difficult to
avoid paying the toll, but now and again 'gay sparks' succumbed to the
temptation to circumvent the barrier, and more often than not finished
up in the ditch.[5] The old toll-keeper stayed on duty until late at night,
emerging from his shelter, nightcap on head and carrying a lantern,
ready to collect the money from the belated and sometimes incoherent
traveller before issuing a ticket and opening the five-bar gate.[6] The
delays which occurred, particularly on Derby Day, were a constant
cause of irritation, and removal of the Figges Marsh gate and others
along the road to Brighton in October 1865 was a source of considerable
satisfaction to the travelling public.

Figges Marsh Gate – Return from the Derby
Illustrated London News, 31 May, 1845

Tooting Old Hall

Until it was surrounded by the newly erected villas in Arnold and Finborough Roads late in the 19th century, the first building to catch the eye on the way to Mitcham was Tooting Old Hall, standing to the right of the road on the future site of Woodley Close, the block of flats erected in the 1930s. The Hall was a typical 18th century brick-built house, three-storeyed and of four bays, with a pantiled mansard rood. Ivy-covered in its old age, it stood in the midst of a pleasant garden with lawns and rose beds encompassed by tall trees.

With justification, *The Queen's London*, published in 1896, described the Hall as a "charming place", and captioned an illustration of it "Defoe's House at Mitcham".[1] The supposed connection with Defoe had evidently been accepted for some time, and was mentioned in an account of the beating of the bounds of Mitcham in May 1879.[2] In the 1880s the house was occupied by a Holborn bookseller by the name of Bumpus,[3] who we can imagine was quite prepared to have his residence

Late 19th-century engraving of Tooting Old Hall

linked with such a distinguished literary figure. (He may even have been responsible for the inscription in gothic script on the front gate, proclaiming that "Defoe lived here in 1688").

Daniel Defoe, the London journalist and novelist whose *Robinson Crusoe* and *Moll Flanders* are still deservedly popular, published over 560 books, pamphlets and journals, many written when he had turned 60 years of age. Described as the father of English journalism, he died in 1731 at the age of 71,[4] and despite the strength of local tradition, proof of his residence on the borders of Mitcham or, indeed, anywhere else in the parish of Tooting, appears non-existent. Certainly by the late 18th century any house Defoe might have occupied on the site near Figges Marsh had disappeared, for in 1784, on what had become a vacant plot, "a corner of Mr. Garrood's field", Tooting vestry erected the Old Hall as a workhouse for the reception of the poor and infirm of the parish.

Morden, in his *History of Tooting-Graveney* set out the story of this establishment in some detail, and there is no need to cover the ground again.[5] Like most parish workhouses, its use for the accommodation of the destitute and homeless ceased after the passing of the Poor Law Amendment Act of 1834, and in 1841 a meeting of Tooting parish resolved that the empty workhouse should be sold by the Board of Guardians of the Poor. The 'Workhouse Garden' and the adjoining 'Workhouse Meadow', both in the possession of the Revd Humphrey Waldo-Sibthorpe, a Mitcham landowner, appear in the Mitcham tithe register of 1846,[6] but the house itself remained in the parish of Tooting until local government boundary revisions at the close of the century brought the whole of the property within Mitcham's jurisdiction.

In March 1855, at a court baron of the manor of Biggin and Tamworth, two plots of recently enclosed common land, lying between the former workhouse and the main road, were granted to George Vaughan and the Revd Greaves. The latter had apparently purchased the workhouse meadow and garden from Waldo-Sibthorpe a short time before.[7] The Hall was demolished after the end of the 1914–18 war, but not before the traditional connection of Defoe with the neighbourhood had influenced the authorities to perpetuate his memory by renaming the

Enclosure of Common Land – Figges Marsh – permitted by Manor of Biggin and Tamworth – Courts held by Thomas E. Penfold esq. following death of James Moore. (Court Rolls at Surrey History Centre)

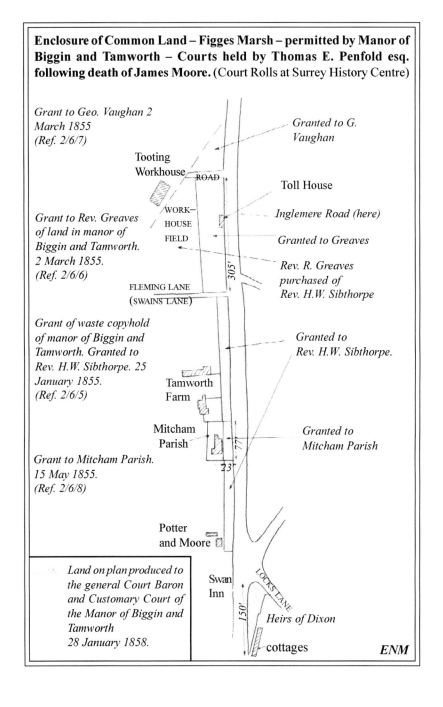

Grant to Geo. Vaughan 2 March 1855 (Ref. 2/6/7)

Granted to G. Vaughan

Tooting Workhouse

ROAD

Toll House

WORK— HOUSE FIELD

Inglemere Road (here)

Grant to Rev. Greaves of land in manor of Biggin and Tamworth. 2 March 1855. (Ref. 2/6/6)

Granted to Greaves

Rev. R. Greaves purchased of Rev. H.W. Sibthorpe

305'

FLEMING LANE

(SWAINS LANE)

Grant of waste copyhold of manor of Biggin and Tamworth. Granted to Rev. H.W. Sibthorpe. 25 January 1855. (Ref. 2/6/5)

Granted to Rev. H.W. Sibthorpe.

Tamworth Farm

Mitcham Parish

77'

Granted to Mitcham Parish

Grant to Mitcham Parish. 15 May 1855. (Ref. 2/6/8)

23'

Potter and Moore

Land on plan produced to the general Court Baron and Customary Court of the Manor of Biggin and Tamworth 28 January 1858.

Swan Inn

LOCKS LANE

150'

Heirs of Dixon

cottages

ENM

Colliers Wood end of Swains Lane Robinson Road, and giving the names Pitcairn, Island, Friday and Crusoe to new roads in north Mitcham.

The boundary between Tooting and Mitcham in the vicinity of Tooting Old Hall had become illogical by the late 19th century. It was almost certainly following a long-defunct channel of the Graveney, and was likely to have been pre-Conquest in date. It had marked the division between the hundreds of Brixton and Wallington since the time of King Alfred, and for close on a thousand years had sufficed to define the parish boundaries for ecclesiastical purposes. As local government evolved in Tudor times it provided the natural boundary for the civil parishes, but now it had become an administrative anomaly. Reorganisation of local government towards the close of Victoria's reign commenced with the transfer of north-eastern Surrey to the newly-formed administrative County of London in 1888, and was followed by the creation of district and parish councils under the Local Government Act of 1894. The London Government Act of 1899 carried the process a stage further, and brought into existence the Metropolitan Borough of Wandsworth, which incorporated the civil parish of Tooting-Graveney. It was quite obvious that the boundary irregularities had to be resolved and, on representation being received from the London County Council, a provisional order was proposed by the Local Government Board under the Local Government Acts 1888 and 1894 altering the county and local government boundaries between London and Surrey. It was generally agreed that it was administratively inconvenient for part of the parish of Tooting-Graveney to remain in Mitcham – then a 'contributory place' within the rural district of Croydon – and after a public enquiry in June 1902 a new boundary was adopted, following the northern fence of the railway line, to the south of properties fronting Longley Road.[8] In April 1903 Tooting Old Hall and the land south of the railway was tranferred to Surrey and Mitcham – a situation which was to remain unchanged until further reorganisation of London government took place in 1965 and the London Borough of Merton came into being.

Swains Farm

Swains Road, or Swain's Lane as it was known until the mid-20th century, leads away from the northern tip of Figges Marsh towards Colliers Wood and the old Roman road to London. It is shown on the first edition of the Ordnance Survey map published in 1816, and provided a route from Colliers Wood via Biggin Farm (later Gorringe Park) to Streatham Lane and beyond, via bridleways and footpaths, to the hamlet of Lonesome and Lower Streatham. Apart from providing farm access to Swains Farm, it seems not to have performed any major function by the middle of the 19th century, and when the railway was constructed from Tooting to Merton Park in 1868 the company only considered it necessary to erect a footbridge.

Swains Farm, on the northern outskirts of the parish, could probably claim considerable antiquity, and its tenants asserted their right to common grazing on Figges Marsh until the 1860s. Lying as it did close to the Tooting border and the new railway, Swains was one of the first of the Mitcham farmsteads to be submerged when London's suburbs expanded at the end of the 19th century. Swain in its various forms had, of course, been a common enough surname for centuries, and occurs, for instance, in charters of Henry VII, where it is rendered as Swynes or Swaynes. The name is interesting and, as we have already suggested, in north Mitcham it may enshrine the memory of an Anglo-Danish settler named Sven or something similar, who had a homestead here before the Conquest.

On the other hand, the farm could once have been the property of Swein who, the Domesday survey tells us, in the time of King Edward held Tooting and Wandworth. In Morris's opinion, Swein might have been Swein of Essex, a kinsman of the king. Yet other possibilities are that the farm derived its name from either William, son of Sweyn, or Robert le Sweyn, both of Morden, whose names appear in the muniments of Westminster Abbey in 1225 and 1296 respectively.[2]

The tithe map of 1847 shows two groups of buildings on or near the site of Swain's Farm. One was a house and cottage with gardens and a barn, occupied by a Thomas Locks together with three plots of "meadow now arable" totalling nearly 16 acres. The other, a smaller holding of approximately 10 acres in the tenure of Richard Brook, included a house and garden, an orchard and a slaughterhouse. Both properties were owned by James Moore. The 1851 census merely recorded Richard Brook living in Swains Lane, describing him as a farmer with roughly 20 acres of land, from which we can conclude that Locks had left, and the two holdings were probably amalgamated. By the time the estate of the late James Moore was auctioned in 1853, however, there had been further changes, and the "homestead", consisting of a house and cottage (which included a dairy) a stable, barn, yard, and piggeries were held on a lease granted to William Harland, a local paint manufacturer.[3] The farm had been let to John Henry Bunce, a market gardener who, with his wife Mary, their four children and their 'house servant' Jane Warner, is listed in the census return for 1861. Ten years later the Bunce family had left for, it would seem, another farm in Merton parish.

Although most of its land had been taken for housing, Swain's Farm survived as a working smallholding until about 50 years ago. Cows were still kept until the early 1930s, and milk was sold retail to callers. The house, which from the exterior appeared to be no older than the mid-19th century, was demolished in 1966.

Figges Marsh, or Tamworth, Farm

Beyond the Figges Marsh milestone the visitor to Mitcham in the mid-19th century would soon have seen on his right another farmhouse, with its associated yard, barns and outbuildings, backed by large rectangular elm-fringed fields and meadows extending back to the west field and old hay furlongs of Mitcham. Beyond, farmland continued without interruption towards Merton and the wooded slopes of Wimbledon Park. The farmstead was that of Figges Marsh Farm,[1] and with the aid of the 25-inch Ordnance Survey map published in 1867, one can see that the farmstead, by this time named Tamworth Farm, straddled what is today the southern entrance and children's playground of Tamworth Farm Recreation Ground. Smaller-scale maps a century earlier also show buildings here, but they are not named.[2] The Greenwoods mark "Fig's Marsh Farm" on their map of Surrey, published in 1823, but when and why the farm acquired the name Tamworth Farm is not known for certain. There seems to have been no connection whatever with the manor of Biggin and Tamworth, and the best one can suggest is that the farm acquired its new name sometime after 1822 (by which time Lord Redesdale's Tamworth House, on the other side of Figge's Marsh had been demolished, and before the mid-1860s. Tamworth Farm was presumably thought to project a better image than the older name, and was undoubtedly preferable to its corruption 'Pig's Marsh Farm'.

James Drewett, writing in the 1920s, recalled what he described as a "real old farmhouse" standing here when he was a boy in the 1860s.[3] This implies that the house itself was at least 100–150 years old, and it is quite possible for it to have dated to the late 16th century, when all over England a great expansion of agriculture took place, with many new farmhouses being built by the rising class of yeoman farmers. The origins of the farm itself probably lie in the Middle Ages, however, and until the latter part of the 19th century it was a copyhold property within the manor of Ravensbury. Colliers Wood House, the grounds of which abutted the fields of Tamworth Farm, was within the same manor and as Jenkingranger its history has been traced back to 1486 through the medium of the court rolls. The field pattern of mainly large, rectangular enclosures, to be seen in the tithe map of 1847, tends to support the assumption that Tamworth Farm post-dated the common west field with its ancient strip holdings, and was a creation of the later Middle Ages or early Tudor period.

Local records show that in the mid-18th century much of the land comprising Figges Marsh Farm was owned by the Waldo family, ancestors of whom were believed to have settled in Mitcham in the 16th century.[4] A clue to the occupancy of the property in the late 1750s is the admission of a Robert Simmons, a 'gardener' (i.e. grower of aromatic and medicinal herbs) to the copyhold tenancy of "two tenements, gardens and appurtenances adjoining ... situated on the west side of ffiggs Marsh", in 1756. The property lay within the manor of Ravensbury, and 'Waldo 1765' is written on the front of the deed. Ten years later, Simmons having died, the tenancy was surrendered to Francis Merritt "of Mitcham, Victualler and his heirs and successors".

Merritt appears elsewhere in local records, (his name is on the Freeholders List for 1764–5, for instance) and is known to have been the licensee of the Nag's Head at Fair Green in the 1760s. The use to which he put the farm is not known, but since Merritt remained at the Nag's Head until his death in the 1780s, Figges Marsh Farm was presumably sub-let.[5]

The property was tenanted by an Edward Pickton in 1805, together with some 52 acres of land rented from Hannah Waldo, widow of Peter Waldo who had died the previous year.[6] Edward was succeeded by John Pickton, but his tenure failed to weather the post-war depression in agriculture.[7] A guide book to Surrey, published in 1823, describes the farm as "Fig's Marsh Farm",[6] and a plan of those parts of the Waldo estate lying within the manor of Ravensbury, prepared in 1825, shows the house and 51 acres to be tenanted by a John Faulks or Foakes.[8] Until 1824 Foakes was resident at The Poplars, a large 18th-century house (to be described later) situated nearer the centre of the village, close by the Swan inn. Pigot's *Directory* for 1839 lists him as John "Folkes" of Figges Marsh and, on the evidence of his being described as a farmer and physic gardener, we are justified in including Foakes among the considerable number of Mitcham landowners who, by the middle of the 19th century, were emulating Potter and Moore and had turned over much of their land to the cultivation of aromatic and medicinal herbs on a commercial scale.

The tenancy of Figges Marsh Farm passed through a succession of hands before the middle of the century. A William Brown was recorded in the 1841 census, but by 1846, when it had become the property of the Revd Humphrey Waldo-Sibthorpe, the farm was worked by William Holland and Isaac Barber.[9] Holland died shortly afterwards, but Barber, a native of Nottingham, continued with his wife Anne as the tenant into the 1860s, by which time it had become known simply as Marsh Farm.[8] Most of the 80-odd acres was arable, and lay to the west of the main London Road between what is now Lavender Avenue and Victoria Road. In all probability the major part of the farm continued to be used for the cultivation of herbs under the partnership of Holland and Barber, and we are told that during the 1860s one of the farm buildings was fitted out as a small distillery for the extraction of essential oils.[3] In

1855, following the death of James Moore and when settlement of the family estate was in the hands of his executors, Waldo-Sibthorpe benefited from a grant of enclosure of "waste, copyhold of the manor of Biggin and Tamworth" extending along the roadside frontage of the farm. This was, in fact, former common land and had been part of the wider expanse of Figges Marsh.[11]

The 1871 Census does not include premises readily identifiable as Tamworth or Marsh Farm, which could mean the buildings were unoccupied or even that the farmhouse had been demolished. Certainly, by the time the second 25 inch to one mile edition of the Ordnance Survey map was published in 1894–6 the old house and most of the outbuildings had gone. The farm has long since passed from living memory and, regrettably, no photographs or drawings of it have found their way into the local illustrations collection of Merton Libraries. Its place was taken by a detached villa, named Tamworth Farm, erected partly on the newly-enclosed land between the old farmstead and the main road.

'Tamworth Farmhouse', 106 London Road, Mitcham (1975).
This late Victorian villa replaced a much earlier farmhouse

The new villa, numbered 106 London Road and built in a style which suggests it dated from the 1870s, has its own place in local history, having for a short time been the residence of James Chuter Ede (1882–1965), later Lord Chuter Ede, Labour Member of Parliament for the Mitcham Division of Surrey from March until November 1923.[12] At the time of his first election, when he was returned with a small majority, he was a young Epsom ex-teacher and secretary of the Surrey Association of Teachers. From 1929 to 1931, and again from 1935 to 1964 he represented the constituency of South Shields. Chuter Ede was Parliamentary Secretary for the Ministry of Education in Churchill's War Cabinet from 1940 to 1945. With R A Butler he was the architect of the 1944 Education Act, and became Home Secretary from 1945–1951 in the Labour government elected after the defeat of Germany. He had also been chairman of Surrey County Council from 1933 until 1937, and was made an honorary freeman of the Borough of Mitcham in 1944. Chuter Ede's house was demolished in 1977, and between 1978 and 1980 Dennis Reeve Close, a small estate of houses and maisonettes providing sheltered accommodation for the elderly, was erected on the site by the London Borough of Merton.

London Road Cemetery and Tamworth Farm Recreation Ground

By the end of World War I farming activity at Tamworth Farm had come to an end, and a substantial acreage was purchased for house building by the new Urban District Council. The population of Mitcham had increased from 15,015 in 1901 to 35,119 in 1921, and the former village was developing rapidly into a small town. It was becoming obvious that the original burial ground around the parish church, already virtually doubled in size by an extension consecrated in 1908, would soon become inadequate, and accordingly a further tract of former farmland, extending back from the London Road with a northern boundary on Victoria Road, was acquired by the Council for a new municipal cemetery. This was duly laid out and, complete with a lodge and chapel, the foundation stone of which was laid in January 1928 by Esmé Heard, wife of George Thomas Heard J.P., the chairman of the Council. The architects were Chart, Son and Reading, and the builders G H Gibson Ltd.

The site of the old farmstead, together with what remained of its fields, also passed into public ownership at this time, thanks to the generosity and foresight of Thomas A Mason of Reigate,[1] proprietor of a firm of sauce and condiment manufacturers, whose factory was at Wandsworth. Passing through Mitcham one day in 1923, Thomas Mason noticed that the farm was for sale, and quite informally broke his journey at the Vestry Hall to ask the clerk to Mitcham Urban District Council, Stephen Chart, if his authority would accept the property as a gift, with £1,000 to put it in order. Mason's only stipulation appears to have been that part of the land should be retained as permanent allotment gardens.[2] The gift was accepted with gratitude, and the donor's wishes have been observed to the present day. A pavilion and bandstand were erected by the Council, and part of the land was used for the construction of Mitcham's first public tennis courts. The distinction was also claimed for Tamworth Farm of being the first public recreation ground in Mitcham to have a court laid out expressly for the game of netball.[3] To these amenities there were subsequently added a seven-rink bowling green and a children's playground.

London Road frontage of Tamworth Recreation Ground in 1967. The line of old hedgerow elms marked the former western margin of Figges Marsh.

Late in 1966 several of the heavily-pollarded elms forming a row which partially screened the pavilion of Tamworth Farm Recreation Ground from London Road, were felled by the parks department as they were considered to have become unsafe. The trees had been a prominent feature of the site for many years and, like a similar row along the eastern margin of Figges Marsh, had most likely originated in the hedges planted in 1801 to divide the common waste from the surrounding private agricultural land. A rough count of the annual rings of one of the trees confirmed that they were well over 150 years old,[4] and already flourishing by the time the Napoleonic Wars ended in 1815. Sadly, all the elms around Figges Marsh had become severely affected by Dutch elm disease by the 1970s, and when the few surviving specimens in front of Tamworth Farm Recreation Ground were removed in 1973 the last visible link with the old farm disappeared.

In the years following the 1939–45 war the formal bedding displays at Tamworth Farm became one of the show pieces of Mitcham, earning high praise for the staff of the parks department of the Borough of Mitcham. For a while the tradition was continued by the London Borough of Merton after 1965. The beds bordered 100 yards or so of the main London Road, and with their glorious splashes of colour lasting from spring through to late autumn, gave pleasure to thousands travelling daily between Mitcham and Tooting. Regrettably standards gradually declined, and restrictions placed on local authorities' expenditure in the 1990s and changed priorities locally resulted in Merton's annual carpet-bedding programme being severely curtailed. In 1998 the beds at Figges Marsh were planted and maintained by the Mitcham Horticultural Society, but this could only be a temporary measure, and the care of the grounds is now placed with contractors.

The Tamworth Farm bandstand, no longer in use, was removed many years ago. The concrete base survived until after the 1939–45 war, but following the abolition of Mitcham Corporation under the reorganisation of London government in 1965 this too was removed. In 1973, the local press reported that the recreation ground chalet had become a 'white elephant' and that closure was considered, but the Council felt obliged to retain it "under the terms of the bequest".[5] For a number of years the chalet restaurant was run successfully by a private caterer holding the premises on a lease. By 1996, however, with its clientele dwindling following closure of the bowling green. and experiencing difficulties in recruiting staff, the future of the chalet café was said to be in the balance.[6]

The Poplars

Although the scale he used is small, a substantial building can be discerned on John Rocque's map of the environs of London dated 1741–5 occupying the site of the inter-war council houses numbered 5–7 and 6–12 Lavender Avenue. No name is given, but the land tax records remove any question as to the building's function, enabling it to be identified as Mitcham's first workhouse, created in 1737 by the adaptation of what had until that time been a gentleman's house. The building reverted to being a private residence around the time of the French Revolution, and during the reign of George IV became a school, a role it was to play, as The Poplars Boarding Academy for Young Gentlemen, until it was demolished in the 1880s.

In 1789, when the building had ceased to shelter the parish poor and was once more a private residence, it was described by Edwards[1] as "a neat white boarded house" belonging to local landowner Peter Waldo, then living at The Elms to the south of the present public library in London Road. One faded photograph of The Poplars has come down to us, dated roughly to about 1870.[2] This shows it to have been five bays wide and three storeys high, weatherboarded after the manner of many of the older Mitcham houses then still standing, and with sliding sash windows and an elegant pedimented front entrance of the type fashionable in the 18th century.

We are helped further in creating a mental picture of the old workhouse and, incidentally, are given an intriguing glimpse of the facilities offered to the inmates, by the Mitcham vestry minutes of November 1737.[3] Having decided that a building should be rented rather than purchased, the vestry (the local government authority of the day), deliberated on "whither the House upon the Marsh belonging to Mr Waldo and now in the Occupation of George Umfreville be proper and convenient and fit to place the Poor together in?". A vote was taken by the customary show of hands, and the answer being in the affirmative with only two dissensions, a committee of ten was appointed to arrange for the "fitting up of the intended House and all other matters relating to the providing of what is fit and convenient for maintaining and employing the Poor that shall be placed therein". Peter Waldo (father of the owner of the house in 1789) agreed to satisfactorily

> "new-rip his House and make good all the Brick-work, Plaistering-work and other Work so as to put the same into Substantial repair ... and to inclose and fence the Ground with a five foot pale and an Arch of Brick in order for a Gate-way both for a Cart and footway over against the Front Door of the House."

New windows were to be fitted, a new chimney constructed in the "great-Room intended for a Work-room" and a "Convenient double necessary-House one for the men and one for the Women". It was left to Waldo to furnish the house "as he shall think proper". A 21-year lease was agreed at a rental of £12 per annum, possession commencing by 5 December 1737.

The workhouse was to have a chequered career in the hands of various managers or 'farmers' (i.e. private contractors) until 1782, when the vestry decided to build a large new workhouse on the far side of Mitcham Common.[4] As soon as this building was ready for occupation the poor were transferred, apparently much to the annoyance of Peter Waldo, who gave expression to his dissatisfaction by withholding payment of his poor rate. A threat of legal proceeding by the vestry was necessary before Waldo could be induced to end his protest.

The location of the old workhouse, bounded in part by the farm yard and herb gardens belonging to James Potter, is indicated by an entry in the vestry minutes for December 1769, in which there is reference to the repair of the "north fence of the workhouse adjoining Mr. Potter's ground", and although no addresses are given (house numbering was, of course, unknown in the village at this period) the land tax books 11 years later confirm the relative positions of the two properties, and both can be identified quite readily on the 25-inch Ordnance Survey map of 1867.

Despite its recent use, Waldo seems to have encountered little difficulty in reletting the former workhouse once the parish's lease had been terminated, but it was, after all, pleasantly situated, facing the London Road and overlooking the southern tip of Figges Marsh. From 1784 until 1786 the house was tenanted by a Miss Warren at a rental of £18 per annum, and subsequent lessees seem to have taken it on an annual basis. When vacant in about 1789 the property was probably refurbished and enlarged, for in 1790 it was re-let to a Mrs Vann at £25 per annum. She stayed for five years and then, in 1795, a long lease of the freehold house, with its outbuildings, yard and grounds, was granted to John Foakes, who made The Poplars his home for 30 years.[5]

It was in about 1825 that the former workhouse assumed a new and what was to be its final role, for like several of the larger houses in Mitcham, it became a private boarding academy for boys. For a brief period the occupier was the Revd Hyam Burns, who had been a curate to the Revd Myers, the vicar of Mitcham who died in 1824.[6] Almost certainly, he was the same Hyam Burns who ran a boys' academy at Park Place, on Commonside West, Mitcham, from 1837 until about 1850. It seems that Burns occupied The Poplars on a sub-lease, for in 1823 the records of the manor of Ravensbury show the copyhold of the property to have been granted to John England Rudd, who held the lease from Hannah Waldo, Peter Waldo's widow.[7] The census of 1841 found The Poplars occupied only by the housekeeper, Mrs Sarah Moss, and her three daughters, but we know that throughout most of the 1840s it was the residence of John Rudd, afforded the status of 'esquire' in the local directories, where he is listed under 'Gentry'.[8] What the tithe register recorded as the "house, offices and garden", covering a modest two roods and one pole, was still in the tenure of Rudd in 1846,[9] whilst ownership had passed to the Revd Humphey Waldo-Sibthorpe, who had inherited the extensive Waldo estate in Upper Mitcham.

By the time the census was conducted in 1851 the schoolmaster at The Poplars was John Spencer. Twenty-three boys were listed as boarders, their ages ranging from eight to 13 years. One came from Demerara, where possibly his parents were living, but the rest were natives of either Middlesex or Surrey, and included several from Mitcham. Among the latter was James Bridger junior, grandson of James Moore.

Spencer's occupancy did not last long, and in 1862 the Post Office *Directory* lists The Poplars with the address of Tamworth Green, and in the hands of Albert Grover. This remained the situation throughout the 1870s and, judging by the comments of several contemporary local historians, Grover's Poplars Academy achieved a reputation as a high class preparatory school. Emma Bartley, whose father was one of the village doctors, remembered the Poplars as "a school for gentlemen's sons", where she believed "the late Lord Radstock was at school".[10] This was, presumably, the son of George Granville Waldegrave, the second Baron Radstock (1786–1857), who had served in the navy during the Napoleonic Wars, and became vice-admiral in 1851.[11] Havelock Ellis, the author, attended The Poplars from 1871–c.1873, and recalled his days there in his autobiography.[12] Grover, he remembered as a kindly headmaster, but "an oddity, a tall middle-aged man, looking much older than his years, with a long grey beard, a bald head" and having "some resemblance to Darwin". Although Ellis felt unable to make "any high claims for the educational methods" employed at The Poplars, the two years he spent there proved profitable enough, and he left at the age of 14 indebted to two masters, Joseph Stevens, who taught French, and Angus Mackay, the assistant English master, both of whose efforts and inspiration he recalled with appreciation and gratitude.

What seems to be the last mention of The Poplars is in the 1882 edition of Kelly's *Directory*, by which time the old wooden building was probably in need of considerable repair. According to Tom Francis,[13] closure of the school was actually brought about by a serious outbreak of scarlet fever. Grover seems to have been the last tenant, and the building had been demolished by the time the survey was being conducted for the 1894 Ordnance Survey Map. As far as is known, the site of The Poplars remained open land until the Urban District Council commenced building its Lavender Avenue and Bordergate Housing Estates in the early 1920s. This was one of the fledgling authority's first ventures into the field of municipal housing, and advantage was taken of the financial assistance available under the provisions of the Housing Act 1919, a measure designed to meet the post-war aim of providing "homes fit for heroes".

POTTER AND MOORE 'PHYSICK' GARDENERS OF MITCHAM

For a little over 150 years, commencing around 1730, the sprawling, populous village of Mitcham lay at the heart of a herb-growing district unique in the history of this country. Foremost amongst its many 'physick gardeners', the excellence of whose perfumery and medicinal products earned world-wide acclaim, were Benjamin Potter and his nephew James Moore, in whose hands the business founded by their families in the reign of George II evolved and prospered in the late 18th and early 19th centuries to become the largest in Britain. Towards the close of Victoria's reign the Mitcham herbal industry declined, hastened, in the case of Potter and Moore, by the death in 1885 of James Moore's natural son, James Bridger, and by the rising value of building land brought about by the expansion of London. The industry also suffered increasingly from competition with overseas growers who, although incapable of matching the excellence of the English product, enjoyed the advantages of low labour costs and cheap land. Today Mitcham peppermint and lavender, like Stilton cheese and Aylesbury duckling, may strictly be misnomers, but the names survive as a mark of quality which has never been surpassed.

More than 2,000 years ago the physicians of ancient Greece relied for their supply of medicaments upon the *rhizotomi*, or root-cutters, a class of people whose occupation was the gathering and sale of wild roots and herbs. They are mentioned by Theophrastus, and most of them were ignorant and superstitious, ascribing magical virtues to the plants they collected. Among the Romans these cullers of simples were termed *herbarii*, or herbalists, and, if we are to believe Pliny, they were a sad set of knaves.[1]

A century and a half ago there was at least one old woman in Mitcham, known as a 'simpler', who managed to obtain a living by gathering medicinal plants, including many common wild flowers still to be found on the Common and uncultivated waste land.[2] Plants are, of course, still an important source of drugs and medicines, but until the advances made in pharmacology during the last century they provided the vital raw material for druggists and chemists. With few exceptions, by the 18th century the supply of wild herbs was quite inadequate to meet the demand from the apothecaries and the medical profession and, where amenable to cultivation in this country, they were produced in the required quantities by the physic gardeners or herb growers. Although the cultivation of medicinal plants was carried on in various parts of England, more land came to be employed in this way in Surrey than in any other county, and nowhere in the kingdom, we are told, was the cultivation of "these very necessary articles in the *materia medica* attended to with so much care and diligence".[3] Until as late as 1850 by far the greater part of the Surrey physic grounds still lay within Mitcham and its neighbouring parishes in the valley of the Wandle.

Lavender, the plant usually associated with Mitcham, although it was not grown here in large quantities until the 19th century, has the ability to flourish in relatively poor soils, and indeed hundreds of acres of the thin chalky soils between Croydon and Sutton remained under cultivation by herbal gardeners until shortly after the first World War. Peppermint, too, was a crop widely grown within and beyond the Mitcham borders, and growers such as the Sprules family at Wallington and James and George Miller at Beddington Corner were enjoying a well-deserved reputation for the quality of their products towards the close of the 19th century, when production in Mitcham was declining sharply.[4]

Romano-British and Saxon farmers alike had been attracted to the fertile loams of the Wandle valley, and from the commentaries surviving from the 18th century it would appear that the land to the southwest and west of Mitcham village centre especially had long been recognised as ideally suited to the cultivation of herbs of all kinds. In particular, there seemed to be a special quality in the soil which imparted to Mitcham lavender a scent peculiarly its own, leading to the districts becoming associated with the production of essences of the finest quality and fragrance. There is mention in the annals of Merton priory to the growing of 'spikings', or lavender, and in 1301 as much as 44 quarters (550 kg) were sold from the priory estates, which included land in Mitcham subsequently farmed by Potter and Moore.[5]

The evidence points to the commercial distillation of herbal essences on a modest scale in Mitcham from the middle of the 18th century, when we first find the names of Potter and Moore associated. Cultivation of medicinal herbs was undoubtedly well-established before then. Members of the Potter family were living in Mitcham in the 17th century, and a William Potter of Mitcham was described as "having the most complete garden for English raised flowers" in a botanical dictionary published in 1728.[6] Henry Potter, a 'gardener' who had a little over four acres in cultivation in both the east and west common fields between 1715 and 1729, was probably cultivating herbs, but the will of John Potter of Mitcham, proved in 1742, describes him specifically as a 'Physick Gardener'. Seven years later John's son Ephraim is said to have founded with William Moore a distillery at Mitcham for the production of lavender water.[7] Their Mitcham lavender water proved to be an immediate favourite with the public of the day, its popularity stemming in part, one suspects, from its value as a masking agent in an age not noted for its high standard of personal hygiene.

We are told by Lysons that in 1752 only a few acres of land in Mitcham were used for the growing of medicinal herbs.[8] Ephraim's son James is said to have been cultivating lavender on a very small scale in 1768 or 1779,[3] but by great care, skill and industry had "so increased his growth, as at the time of his deathe ... to be considered the first grower in England and to have amassed a competent fortune". Ephraim Potter died in about 1773 (the date of his will), and was succeeded by his son James, whose farm and distillery overlooking Figges Marsh, where Eveline Road is today, was to become a showpiece of repute well before the end of the century.

Potter is unlikely to have been the only herb grower in this part of Mitcham at this time, and there is a record of the admission of Robert Simmons, a 'gardener', to a copyhold tenancy of Ravensbury in 1756. No map accompanies the deeds, but the property, which comprised two tenements with gardens and appurtenances was, like Potter's, situated on the west side of "ffiggs Marsh".[8]

In 1789 Potter's establishment was visited by James Edwards, compiling his guide for travellers on the Brighton road.[8] He described the farmhouse as "the residence of Mr. James Potter, whose Botanical Gardens are very extensive, and has works here for extracting the essence of all his botanical herbs. It is remarkable," added Edwards (always alert for snippets of information to interest his readers), "that on Mr. Potter's sinking a well for the use of his works near 200 feet, no water was found; but sinking it something lower, a spring broke up with great force, and, in a few minutes space, rose to the top, and ran over; and it now continues nearly full. The ground consisted of different stratums, and at a great depth were found perfect oyster shells, periwinkle shells etc".[10] Potter's distillery demanded a supply of water far in excess of the capacity of the average shallow well then in common use in Mitcham, and the sinking of this borehole, the first natural artesian well recorded in the village, typifies the progressive attitude which carried him head and shoulders above contemporary growers.

By modern standards Mitcham was still a relatively small village at the close of the 18th century, and intermarriage between members of the families of Potter and Moore was commonplace. Thus it came about that when James Potter died in 1799 the business passed to his nephew, James Moore, then in his 30th year. By 1796 physic gardeners occupied about 250 acres of land in Mitcham, of which 100 acres were devoted to the cultivation of peppermint "much used in making a cordial well-known to the dram-drinkers".[8] The next six years saw a remarkable expansion in the extent of the "garden grounds", as they were called in parish records, and by March 1802 a further 240 acres of former meadow, pasture and arable land, including the greater part of the open common fields, were used for the purpose.[11] War with France, and the consequent disruption of trade with continental growers must have stimulated home production, but the reputation of Mitcham as a source of the finest essences had been established well before the outbreak of hostilities. How far the subsequent expansion in the garden grounds can be attributed to James Moore alone it is difficult to tell, but for the next 50 years he was to dominate the Mitcham scene.

The son of Ann Potter and Benjamin Moore, a calico print cutter, James became an outstanding personality in the village. By repeated purchases of land he increased very considerably the extent of the estate inherited from his uncle, the most notable being his acquisition in 1804 of a substantial part of the Mitcham property of the late John Manship, an East India merchant.[12] In 1805 James Malcolm found Moore cultivating

> "near 500 acres in physical and agricultural pursuits; which, when the value of land so near to the metropolis, and amidst so many manufactories, and the residences of gentlemen of large fortune is considered, must be deemed an extensive estate".

The deep loams and brickearths overlying the Wandle gravels were, as we have seen, particularly suited to the cultivation of medicinal plants, and in the hands of Moore yielded crops in abundance, earning him the unstinted acclamation of the farming world. The methods he adopted were labour intensive, and with James Arthur, another Mitcham grower, who farmed over 300 acres from New Barns Farm on Commonside East, Moore employed a substantial proportion of the local population, men, women and children. The Mitcham herbal industry in fact provided the mainstay of the local economy throughout the first half of the 19th century, but with Moore's death in February 1851 at the age of 81, the era began to come to an end. When he died, the spreading network of railways was already facilitating the spread of London's suburbs, and within 30 years the demand for land and the growing availability of cheap imported herbs combined to render the physic gardens of Mitcham uneconomic and large scale cultivation ceased.

 By far the most complete description of Potter and Moore's distillery and farming methods in the early 19th century is to be found in Malcolm's *Compendium of Modern Husbandry*, written largely during a survey of Surrey conducted at the request of the Board of Agriculture, and published in 1805. Malcolm, described impressively on the title page of his book as "Land Surveyor to their Royal Highnesses the Prince of Wales, and the Dukes of York and Clarence", referred to "my friend James Moore Esq." as "pre-eminently distinguished" in the cultivation of medicinal herbs, and it is obvious that his account is based on much more than a fleeting visit to Mitcham.

The land cultivated by Moore was of varying quality, some of it being very stiff and moist, whilst other parts were dry and gravelly. The weight and quality of the yields achieved owed much to his practice of deep ploughing, regardless of the nature of the soil or crop. To keep the land in good heart he insisted that it was heavily manured, 20 large cartloads of the strongest rotten dung to the acre being considered the minimum required per annum. None of the fields was permitted to lie fallow, and cropping was continuous, with constant hand-weeding and hoeing to ensure the land was kept clean.

Moore maintained four wagon teams, each of four very powerful horses, in his stables. Two, and often three of these teams were on the road to London simultaneously, all the year round, taking herbs, straw or other produce to the markets, and returning with dung from the London stables and night soil from St George's Fields. In the farmyard at Figges Marsh Malcolm counted no fewer than 12 carts of different sizes, five wagons, and a timber carriage. Besides the necessary stabling, the buildings included wagon and cart "lodges", various barns, a "counting-house" or office to which was attached a dry warehouse, and, nearby, a large still-room containing five coal-fired copper stills capable of producing 20 tuns of spirit or oil in 24 hours. Outside the still-room was a large horse-mill and, a short distance away, a drying-house divided, according to Malcolm, into two "apartments" each having coal-fired furnaces, the hot gases from which were conducted through a system of flues beneath canvas-covered frames upon which the herbs were placed for drying. Above the frames was a loft for storing the freshly harvested herbs pending drying. At the rear of the stables and barns was the rickyard, in the upper corner of which Moore had astutely located his timber yard, with a carpenter, wheeler and blacksmith's shop. Here, Malcolm commented, "this essential part of the economy of the farm is carried on under his eye, and without that loss of time and inconvenience attending the sending everything from home to each of these professional people".

Ephraim Potter's old house is indicated on John Rocque's somewhat inaccurate maps of the mid-18th century, and is probably the small house to be seen in a sepia-wash drawing by Buckler dated 1827.[13] Two bays wide and two storeys in height, the front elevation was of brick, but the flank wall was weatherboarded and the gable end shows the exposed timbering of the end roof-truss. The building could well have dated to the end of the 17th century, and was demolished sometime before the 1860s. Moore evidently built himself a new farmhouse soon after inheriting the business. It was very much in the fashion of the typical early 19th-century villa, examples of which are still fairly common in the suburbs of south London, although in the immediate locality Elm Lodge and part of Mitcham Court, both facing the Cricket Green are the only ones to survive in anything like their original form. Upon Moore having purchased the lordship of the manor of Biggin and Tamworth in 1804,[14] the villa became the 'Manor House', a name which it retained until it was demolished some 90 years later. It was described, with some exaggeration, as an "elegant mansion ... the present residence of James Moore Esq." in 1823.[15] Only two illustrations of it are known, one being that by Buckler referred to above, and the other a somewhat indistinct photograph entitled "The Old Manor House", and dated c. 1880.[16] Both show a substantial two-storeyed house of five bays, with a centrally placed entrance doorway sheltered by a flat-roofed portico supported by Doric columns. The slated roof, with a wide eaves overhang and paired soffit brackets, was fashionably low-pitched, and finished with a central lead flat. To the right, both illustrations show a small house, which we assume had been Ephraim Potter's home, and a weatherboarded barn, topped with a clock and a bell-turret.

By the mid-19th century Moore was farming 543 acres of land in Mitcham, 362 of which he owned himself. All but 100 acres of this extensive farm was arable, the rich black loam to the west of the village centre in particular being given over largely to the cultivation of herbs. For reasons which are unknown, Moore never acquired outright possession of the Manor House itself or its extensive outbuildings. In 1805 the freehold house, together with the farm buildings, yards and garden, and 51 acres of land were held by Moore as a tenant of Mrs Hannah Waldo,[17] and the records of the tithe commutation survey, conducted five years before his death, show the "proprietor" of the property to have been the Revd Humphrey Waldo-Sibthorpe. In his later years, when presumably in semi-retirement, Moore seems to have lived away from Mitcham, for the census records indicate that in the 1840s and early '50s the Manor House was occupied by two of Moore's daughters, Jemima Scriven, described as of independent means and

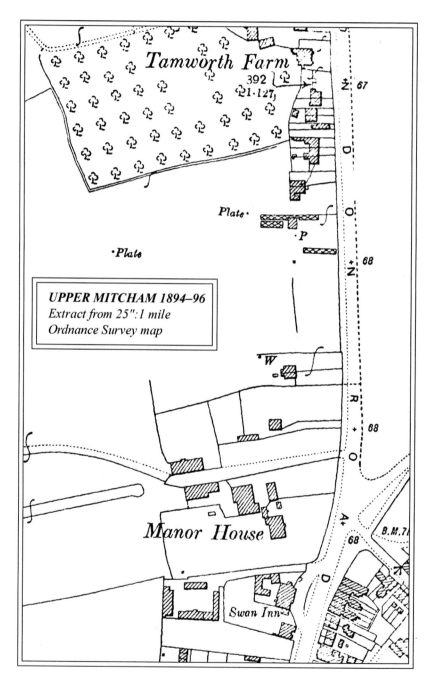

Tamworth Farm

392
1·127

Plate·

·P

·Plate

UPPER MITCHAM 1894–96
Extract from 25″:1 mile
Ordnance Survey map

·W

Manor House

Swan Inn

B.M.7

living on an annuity, and her married half-sister, Charlotte Matilda née Cooper, wife of Thomas Owen, with two servants and Henry Owen, a nephew.[18] Under the terms of Moore's will, dated March 1841, Jemima Scriven was to have use of the house till she married, which she did, in December 1851, taking as her husband the Revd Daniel de Boudry, incumbent of Salesbury near Blackburn.

No portraits of James Moore are known, but his image lives on in many ways. In the vestry minutes of Mitcham his bold flourish of a signature appears year after year, and there is no doubting the influence he wielded over local affairs. A comparatively wealthy man, he purchased the chapel at the eastern end of the north aisle of the old parish church in 1813 when its need of maintenance became an embarrassment to the owners, the Worsfolds of Hall Place, Mitcham. When rebuilding of the church itself commenced in August 1819 Moore bore part of the cost, and as "The Proprietor" laid a foundation stone which can still be seen in the west wall of what became known as 'the Major's Chancel'.[19] It was here, 50 years later, that his widowed daughter Jemima de Boudry willed she should be buried.

Although like many with the financial means, James Moore avoided service in the Royal Surrey Militia by finding a substitute when his name was drawn in the ballot in 1799,[20] he did not shirk his duty at the outbreak of the second Napoleonic War in 1803. With invasion believed imminent, the whole country sprang to arms, and the Loyal Mitcham Volunteer Infantry Corps was formed, with James Moore as its major commandant. Essentially a home defence unit, the corps remained embodied for the rest of the War, Moore being the commanding officer for the whole period.[21] The tablet to his memory, placed in the church by his daughters, records that for many years he was "Major Commandant" of the local military forces.

That Moore could be a stern task master there also seems to be little doubt. Known by many as "the old Major", he was remembered by one old resident, years after his death, as an imposing figure on a grey horse – "the King of Mitcham". "Major Moore in his day was a man of great authority" recalled another old man, "and his word was law".[2] Moore's overseer for many years was Ben Marchant, landlord of the

Horse and Groom in Manor Road. Marchant, a stalwart six feet four inches in height, "straight as a gun barrel and as strong as an ox", was a familiar figure on Moore's land, and "might be seen any day stalking in the fields with a long hoe in his hand as he saw that his men kept at their work".[22] Until the mid-19th century much of the open east common field of Mitcham, and indeed most of the enclosed land lying between the Common and the hamlet of Lonesome on the Streatham border, was either in Moore's ownership, or was held by him as a tenant of other landowners.[23] Tamworth (or 'Thomer') Lane, which gave access to the east fields from the south-east, was gated to prevent damage to crops by livestock straying from the Common, where a handful of parishioners still claimed grazing rights. Mitcham Great Wood, at the foot of Pollards Hill, was part of Moore's estate and here, as on the rest of his land lying to the north-east of the Common, shooting rights were jealously guarded. His gamekeeper, William Temple, was installed in a little thatched cottage at the edge of the Little Wood off Tamworth Lane.

In many respects, James Moore can be seen very much as a man of his time, a veritable John Bull of a character, sturdy and independent, in the best yeoman tradition. Much of his financial success and even social standing came from sheer hard graft and astuteness. One cannot but wonder, however, if he was ever fully accepted into the older village aristocracy of squire and parson, personified in the Cranmer and Myers families. His amorous affairs certainly do not bear close examination – *droit de seigneur* seems to have been his dictum – and his eldest son and heir never assumed his patronym, whilst at least two other sons and his three daughters were the offspring of three or four other alliances. Be this as it may, Moore's attention to his public duties appears utterly creditworthy, and he was for many years a deputy lieutenant of the County, and deeply involved in the affairs of the parish church and the vestry.

In a cynical age one tends to view with some reservation the inscription to James Moore's memory in the church, eulogizing him as "a friend of the poor, ever accessible and nobly generous to all that knew him". It cannot, however, be denied that this view of him was held by many of his contemporaries, and on 14 February 1817, when the post-war depression was bearing heavily on the parish, Moore, then one of the overseers of the poor, was publicly thanked by the vestry, it being minuted that

> "It being very necessary in that times like the present the affairs of the Parish should be managed with discretion as well as with humanity, particularly as it respects the distribution of Parochial Rates,

> Resolved:

> That James Moore Esq., by his unwearied attention to the interests of the Parish of Mitcham, by the proper inspection of every case which comes before the Vestry appears to be guided by a sense, no less of duty to the proprietors of lands and tenements within the Parish than of compassionate consideration for the necessities of applicants who are right objects of relief, and is therefore justly entitled to the unanimous thanks and approbation of this meeting".[11]

The tribute may have been somewhat extravagant, but for all that it does carry a ring of sincerity.

Under the terms of Moore's will, dated 1841, James Bridger, his natural son, inherited both the lordship of the manor of Biggin and Tamworth and ownership of the firm of Potter and Moore.[24] On 29 August 1853 in accordance with the instructions of the executors, and presumably to enable Moore's numerous and generous legacies to be settled, the estate was offered for sale by auction by Crawters at Garraways Coffee-House in 'Change Alley, off Cornhill. The sale particulars were addressed to "Capitalists, Freehold Land and Building Societies, Market Gardeners, Medical Herb Growers, Trustees and others".[25] The precise outcome of the auction has not been ascertained, but 350 acres of land "nearly all freehold" and lordship of the manor passed ultimately into the possession of Bridger. Five years later he had moved with his family into the Manor House, and it was to remain his home for nearly 30 years.[26]

Bridger was already a farmer and herb grower in his own right at the time of his father's death, and was living with his wife Rachel (née Holden), their children and servants in a house to the north of the Buck's

Head in Upper Mitcham.[27] He seems to have maintained things very much as they had been under his late father's management, and Potter and Moore's herbal distillery was to remain fully operational until the mid-1880s. James Drewett recalled the Manor House and the adjacent farmstead, so familiar in his boyhood in the 1860s, as always redolent of peppermint and lavender essences, the scent of which emanated from the stills. The largest of Mitcham's several distilleries, it was still the show place of the village and a perennial source of fascination to the Epsom racegoers, many of whom stopped at the nearby Swan inn for refreshment or a change of horses. Here could be seen and heard the accompaniments incidental to village and farm life – the blacksmith, carpenter, wheelwright and repairing shop, the flail and threshing floor, pig yard, barns, store sheds, the huge distilling coppers, vats and large drying stoves, and the great horse-propelled wooden cogwheel to pump water into the big storage tank which supplied the distillery. High above the counting house was the old Major's clock, set in the turret of the barn facing London Road, from whence it struck the hours and chimed the quarters.[28]

In the 1871 census returns the premises near the Swan appear as "Biggin Farm", evidently having adopted the name of the old farmstead off Streatham Road, the house of which had by this time been demolished, and its stables and outbuildings been modified to meet the needs of the household at the new Gorringe Park House. Under Bridger the firm of Potter and Moore was recorded as having 305 acres under cultivation, and employing some 40 or so men and boys. Towards the end of the 19th century Walford found Mitcham still remarkable for the extent to which roses and other flowers were cultivated.[29] "In Summertime", he said, drawing perhaps a little on earlier writers, "the air is perfumed by whole fields of roses, lavender and sweet and pleasant herbs; and probably there is not in all the Kingdom a single parish on which the wholesale druggists and distillers of the metropolis draw more largely for their supplies". Walford was, we now know with hindsight, describing a Mitcham already fast receding into history, for the years 1886–88 saw the sale of the extensive Bridger estate, and with it the distillery which, for nearly a century and a half, had been at the very heart of the firm founded by Ephraim Potter and William Moore in 1749.[7]

In May 1885, within three weeks of each other, both James Bridger and his old foreman, who had served the firm faithfully for over 50 years, died. The *Croydon Advertiser*, reporting their deaths added, as if to reassure its readers, "The show goes on as usual. The same old still, storehouse and barn, not forgetting the old clock, whose age the local watchmaker has failed to discover ..." Sadly, with the passing of the two old gentlemen, Mitcham was never the same. Benjamin Potter Moore Bridger, the eldest of James Bridger's six sons, who might have continued the family business, had died without a male heir in 1870. On Bridger's own death the business of distilling essential oils, already in a state of near failure, was left to his surviving children, together with the Mitcham estate.[30] The beneficiaries, well aware of the declining profitability of home-grown herbs, and influenced by the value of so much building land on the outskirts of London, divided the estate and put it up for auction. The distillery passed to the Armfield family, into which his eldest daughter, Elizabeth, had married,[31] and it was from them that it was acquired by W. J. Bush, founder of the company of that name.[7]

Bush died in 1889, but his firm remained in Mitcham for over half a century, drawing supplies of lavender and peppermint from ever farther afield as the London suburbs spread relentlessly into rural Surrey. The name and goodwill of Potter and Moore were preserved by W J Bush & Co, who established a special perfumery department and continued the distillation of lavender and other herbs under the original name.[32] In 1968 W J Bush & Co merged with two other companies to form Bush Boake Allen, then the world's largest supplier of flavours and perfumes, with an annual turnover of £20 million. Reorganisation of the production and marketing was to follow amalgamation, and the Potter and Moore section of the group became part of the DeWitt International Organisation, specialising in the manufacture of toiletries. The Potter and Moore name continues to be used, but there is no longer any connection with Mitcham.

After the sale of the Bridger estate the Figges Marsh distillery was dismantled preparatory to demolition of the farm buildings and redevelopment of the site. Some of the stills were re-erected at J & G Miller's premises at Beddington Corner.[33] When the old major's counting house and store was demolished, the bells were salvaged as mementoes and donated to the parish council, who hung them in the tower of the new Vestry Hall, built on the Cricket Green in 1887.[2] As in so many other instances, Mitcham Corporation subsequently treated these links with the community's past with incredible indifference, and the bells have long since disappeared, probably sold for their value as scrap. A limestone block set in the boundary wall of the yard of the Swan, inscribed "N & C" and "1890", probably marked the first stage of redevelopment of the site of the Manor House and the farm yard. Today the land on which Moore's house stood is covered by two terraces of shops erected in 1899, whilst the site once occupied by the distillery and farmyard is now beneath the houses and bungalows numbered 1–13 and 2–12 Eveline Road.

Site of Potter and Moore's premises, London Road, Mitcham,
seen from Renshaw's Corner (1970)

RENSHAW'S CORNER

The Oxtoby Houses, or "The Chestnuts"

Overlooking the southern tip of Figge's Marsh and set well back from Streatham Road behind a broad lawn and gravel drive of impressive dimensions, stands a group of five Georgian houses which, although individually of no great architectural merit, are collectively of acknowledged group value. To the credit of the former owners, John F. Renshaw and Co. Ltd., they were maintained in excellent condition for over 60 years, and still lend character to part of Mitcham known for three-quarters of a century as 'Renshaw's Corner.' On various occasions the houses have been modified internally and provide attractive self-contained accommodation for five separate households. Their importance as a visual amenity received official recognition 50 years ago with listing under the provisions of the Town and Country Planning Act, and they are now classified Grade II.

Oldest in the group, and forming the dominant element, is a three-storeyed, basemented building of six bays in length, originally constructed as two houses. It is a typical example of local vernacular architecture in the first half of the 18th century, but is difficult to date closely in the absence of documentary evidence. Stylistically, if they were in the metropolis, the two houses could easily be from the time of George I or George II, for their window frames are not set deep in the reveals as in later 18th-century houses, and the discreet use of red bricks as an embellishment to door and window openings is more in keeping with the beginning, rather than the middle, of the period. Mitcham, however, was in rural Surrey when these houses were built, and, allowing for a degree of provincial lag, we should therefore think more of the 1740s rather than the 1720s.

Reporting on the houses in 1969, Anthony Quiney, of the Greater London Council's Architect's Department, commented;

> "The houses appear on the map of Surrey published about 1768 which had been surveyed by John Rocque. The scale of this map, two inches to one mile, is sufficient to show the central, original

part quite adequately fronting the road to Streatham near the junction with the road to Tooting and which divides it from Pig's Marsh as it was marked there. In a previous survey by Rocque published in 1748 showing the environs ten miles around London to a scale of 1¼" to one mile the site appears to be occupied by three much smaller buildings. At that time the road to Tooting had not been made along the west side of Figge's Marsh and in consequence it is more difficult to locate the correct site. Tentatively one may conclude that Renshaw's Corner was built at some time between the respective surveys for the maps published in 1748 and 1768. The style of the original part of the building would appear to confirm such a conclusion."[1]

In accordance with the fashion prevailing throughout the Georgian period, the roofs are concealed from view behind a front parapet, and in order to avoid an inordinately high ridge or resort to a flat roof, the device of an 'M' configuration of trusses was adopted, with a transverse valley. This strategy was, however, only necessary in the case of the left hand, or northern house of the pair, since its partner is merely of one bay in depth. The accommodation provided internally is therefore not identical, but to an extent what the northern house gains in depth its partner achieves in width. These houses, one feels sure, were built to meet specific requirements rather than purely speculatively. The builder nevertheless succeeded in maintaining a semblance of that symmetry which was then considered the height of good taste. Close inspection shows the stock brickwork of the front elevation to be laid exclusively in header bond, a rather unusual method of construction normally reserved for quality work. Also interesting is the contrasting treatment of the front doors, the one encased in a bulky porch and clearly intended to impress, and the other protecting callers by a simple canopy, but boasting brackets, each embellished with the likeness of a cherub.

At opposite ends of what we assume to be the original building stand two additions, the one a little house dating perhaps to the latter part of the 18th century, and the other, to the left, a single-storey extension of about 1850. To the rear, discreetly hidden from public view, a motley assortment of extensions may complicate understanding of the evolution of the building, but speaks of efforts to meet the changing needs of successive residents. Similar objectives must have lain behind adaptations to the interiors, but the 18th century character of the main part of the building was not lost in the process, and many of the rooms retain original wooden panelling, dentilled cornices and period fireplaces giving them a distinctive charm.

The first reliable documentary references to these houses are in the poor rate books for the parish, the earliest of which is dated 1756 and gives the names of Samuel Oxtoby and Nathaniel Myers as the owner-occupiers, a category which also included leaseholders. Both were members of families prominent in the parish throughout the 18th century; the Myers family owned land and houses in Lower Mitcham, and were related by marriage to James Cranmer, lord of the manor and squire of Mitcham, whilst the Oxtobys owned property near the Upper Green and elsewhere in the village. The menfolk of both families regularly attended meetings of the vestry, and in their turn held various offices. Samuel was a master carpenter by trade, and with his two sons ran a sizeable building firm.[2] It seems likely that Oxtoby and Sons were responsible for the erection of the two houses central to the Renshaw's corner group and that the more prestigious house was the one in which Nathaniel Myers resided.

Samuel Oxtoby's will, dated 1761 and proved in 1768, shows that he left to his sons John and Samuel two "freehold messuages or tenements fronting Figge's Marsh". John, the elder son, who was brother-in-law to James Moore through his marriage to Harriet Moore, received the house in which their father had lived, whilst the house left to Samuel ("lately purchased from John Ward") was in the occupation of a Mrs Rudduck. Samuel Oxtoby senior willed that his widow, "Roseman" should have use of the "best chamber" in his house and the furniture therein for the rest of her life, and also two freehold houses in Church Lane. John and Samuel were left "all their father's carpenter's trade" and his stock of tools and wood, "the business to continue in partnership in the same premises as now".[3] Roseman Oxtoby survived her husband by a quarter of a century, during which time the Myers remained her neighbours. In her will, proved in 1792, she made various bequests, including one of £2 12 0d per annum to buy bread for the poor of the parish[4] but the bulk of her estate passed to her two sons.

The lease of Nathaniel Myers' old house may have expired towards the end of the 18th century, and the land tax records show John Oxtoby senior in residence in 1793.[1] By 1796 tax was being paid by Samuel Oxtoby, and the freehold was in the possession of John Oxtoby junior in 1825. Fifty years later the northernmost of the two houses, then let to a William Prudence, was in the hands of the trustees of Samuel John Oxtoby.[5] It is believed that it was sold shortly before 1850.[1]

Of the actual occupants in the intervening years little is really known apart from their names, and even then, variations in spelling and gaps in the archive hamper the compilation of a complete list. A James Window seems to have been living at the southern house between 1808 and 1815, and Elizabeth Window continued in occupation until 1827. Their daughter was probably the Elizabeth Mary Window who, in 1820, married the Revd Richard Cranmer, then living at The Canons. In 1824 Richard was instituted vicar of Mitcham, and the couple moved to the newly-built vicarage opposite the parish church in 1826. The tenant or lessee from 1828 to the 1830s was a William Davis, but only Mrs Mary Davis and her four children and servants were recorded in the 1841 census return. By then tenure of the northern house had passed into the hands of Frances Kallender, a lady of independent means, who resided in the house with her family and two servants.[6] The Post Office *Directory* for 1845 was listing a Miss Kallender, and in 1846 the tithe commissioners' surveyors recorded Mary Kallender as the owner-occupier. The Kallenders were typical of a succession of middle-class households who subsequently occupied the house next door until the end of the century, and whose names are to be found in the local directories. Frederick Armfield, the son of one of these families, married Gertrude Elizabeth Bridger, a daughter of James Bridger who, as we have seen, inherited the lordship of the manor of Biggin and Tamworth and became the proprietor of Potter and Moore, following the death of James Moore in 1851.[7] There is also a tradition that the little house to the right of the two larger houses at Renshaw's Corner was once a dower house, but by whom it was occupied has not been ascertained.[8]

In the days before adequate educational facilities were provided by the local authorities and religious organisations, parents were obliged to make the best provision they could for the education of their children. Those fortunate enough to possess the means sent them either to private day schools or boarding establishments, of which there were a large number in the Home Counties. Half a dozen or so existed simultaneously in Mitcham in the 19th century, and at some time in their histories several of the larger houses in the village were used as private academies. The Oxtobys' old house was a typical example, and from the early 1850s until the mid-1880s it was used to accommodate a very select boarding school for girls aged from about six to 13 run by the Misses Rosina and Eliza Spong.[9] Dressed in their Sunday best, clutching their bibles and prayer books, the 'crocodile' of rather haughty young ladies on their way to and from the parish church was a familiar sight in the village. The youthful James Drewett, then one of the village lads, was obviously fascinated, and still recalled the vision 60 years later when writing his memoirs of Old Mitcham.[10]

The houses at Renshaw's Corner were known collectively as The Chesnuts (sic) throughout much of the latter half of the 19th century,[11] and when sale details were prepared in 1896 they were described as freehold, and let to Miss Bullock. Two years later, in 1898, the same property was offered for sale by auction as The Chestnuts – "two capital old-fashioned residences", standing in grounds comprising about two acres.[12] Lot 1, Samuel Oxtoby's old house, was "pleasantly situated with a timbered green in front, traversed by a carriage drive from Streatham Road" (the auctioneers felt no need to comment that a large part of this green had been enclosed from the common land surrounding Figges Marsh). The accommodation comprised six bedrooms on the upper floors, and on the ground floor a "Lofty School Room", 24 feet by 16, in addition to the two sitting-rooms, kitchen and usual domestic offices. The school room extension of 1850 still survives as the lounge of No. 1 Renshaw's Corner.

Lot 2, the larger house, was a far grander affair. In 1861 it had been the residence of William Cohen, a silk merchant, and ten years later the occupant was John Flearwell, a dealer in hides. In addition to six

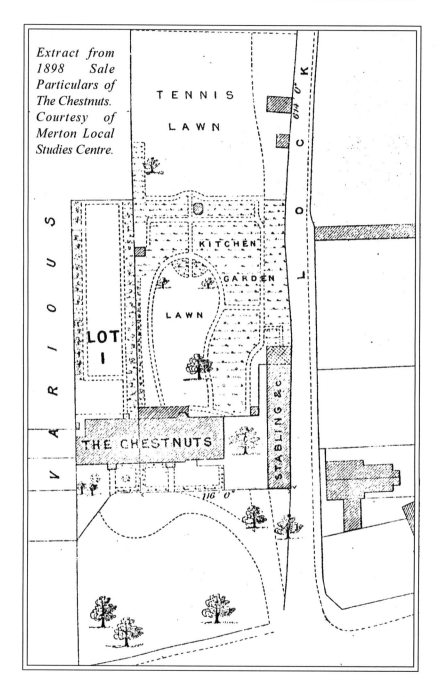

Extract from 1898 Sale Particulars of The Chestnuts. Courtesy of Merton Local Studies Centre.

TENNIS LAWN

KITCHEN GARDEN

LAWN

LOT I

THE CHESTNUTS

STABLING &c.

bedrooms, there were on the first floor day and night nurseries and a bathroom with a "Roman bath" having a marble rim, whilst downstairs there were the drawing room, dining room and morning room. Behind the house was to be found a range of outbuildings comprising coachhouses, stabling, harness rooms, hay lofts, chicken houses etc., running parallel with Lock's Lane. Also to the rear were the gardens, a tennis court and a paddock.

After the auction, part of The Chestnuts was occupied by James Pain and Sons Ltd, the world-famous firework manufacturers who, in 1872, had moved their factory from Brixton to Eastfields.[13] Oxtoby's old house was retained for domestic occupation by Philip, one of James Pain's three sons, whilst the firm took the right-hand and larger house for offices. Philip Pain turned the former schoolroom into a billiards room, and his housekeeper Mrs Piper and her husband occupied rooms to the rear and to the left of the house. Following the death in 1918 of his brother, James Charles, Philip assumed control of the business. A

The houses at Renshaw's Corner, Streatham Road, Mitcham (1966)

bachelor, he seems to have lived very much for his work, concentrating his time and ability on the many ramifications of the family business. Philip Pain did not take any active part in public affairs, but had the reputation of dispensing charity freely. He had been in indifferent health and a semi-invalid for some time when, in April 1926, at the age of 56, he unexpectedly suffered a fatal heart attack whilst at work. He was buried in the family grave in Mitcham parish churchyard.

Soon after Philip Pain's death the company's offices were moved back to London and The Chestnuts was sold. The purchasers were John F. Renshaw and Co. Ltd., manufacturers of marzipan and bakers' confectionery, who in 1920 had bought the former tennis ground and paddock on which to relocate their works, then in cramped accommodation at Battersea.[14] They retained the 18th-century houses, but within a very few years of the purchase Renshaws erected a fine new factory in Lock's Lane.

Lock's Lane and Eastfields Road

James Edwards' map of around 1789, published with his *Companion from London to Brighthelmston,* shows Lock's Lane, un-named, leading away from the southern tip of Figges Marsh in a south-easterly direction towards "Mitcham Common Field", then covering the area known today as Eastfields. The field itself, largely unenclosed and divided into the long narrow strips typical of a medieval open field system, commenced at a point where the present Carew Road meets Lock's Lane. Here a gate across the road barred cattle from straying on or off the field, which extended from Sandy Lane to the left and Baker Lane on the right, to as far as Meopham Road in the north-east. Remarkably, one fragment of this relic of the ancient field still remains under cultivation today, in the guise of the Eastfields allotment gardens.

Lock's Lane is marked by name on the 1867 Ordnance Survey map, and is said to have been so called after Lock's Farm, which stood near the beginning of the lane at the Figges Marsh end. James Drewett, writing of his memories of Mitcham in the 1860s, remembered on the corner with Lock's Lane what he believed were "the remains of an old wayside inn, afterwards used as a cottage".[1] When the tithe survey was conducted in 1846 the somewhat humble farm buildings were recorded as consisting of a yard and buildings, the map showing them located on the southwestern side of the lane. The site is now occupied by Swan Autos and a small office block, the Blenheim Business Centre, numbered 14–24 Lock's Lane. The farmhouse itself seems from the map to have been quite small, either standing at the end of a short terrace of cottages which abutted the farmyard, or else comprising part of what had once been a slightly larger house. Whatever the exact situation in the mid-1840s, the rest of this building was separately occupied. In reality, the 'farm' was a smallholding of some 13 acres of predominantly arable land worked by Thomas Craig, a tenant of Samuel James Oxtoby. Thomas may have taken over the tenancy as recently as 1846 for the Post Office Directory for Mitcham in 1845 only lists a James Craig, described as a "farmer", but unfortunately does not give a precise address. Six of Thomas Craig's fields were unenclosed strips lying either in the common field itself or the adjoining Short Bolstead, another large open field. In addition, he rented an enclosure known as The Five Acres, later to be occupied by John F Renshaw & Co's factory, together with a meadow extending along the southwestern side of Lock's Lane as far as the field gate.

Craig's tenure of Lock's Farm proved of short duration, and he is not listed in the 1851 directory. James Drewett recalled what he described as "the old farmhouse" in Lock's Lane, then in the occupation of a Mr Tilley, but he evidently knew nothing of its history. The Craig family appear not to have left Mitcham, for the name recurs in various contexts over the next 100 years or so, and at least two members of the Craig family worked at the firework factory established by James Pain at Eastfields in 1872. (A J.D. Craig was factory manager from the 1890s until after the 1914–18 war).

The corner plot opposite Lock's Farm and fronting Streatham Road had been occupied by the houses, now known collectively as Renshaw's Corner, since the mid-18th century. As we have seen in the previous chapter, the gardens, a tennis lawn and paddock extended back down the north-eastern side of the lane, and were offered for sale by auction in 1898.[2] Some 20 years later the new owners, James Pain and Sons, sold the land behind the houses to John F Renshaw and Co Ltd.

Founded in 1898 by John F. Renshaw, the company had started life in a small office and storeroom at Great Portland Street. Renshaw had commenced manufacturing marzipan having seen it being produced in Germany, and steady expansion of the business soon dictated removal, first to larger premises in Fenchurch Street in 1906, and then again in 1912 to an old disused factory at Battersea.[3] In 1920, when trade was once more in full swing, yet another move became necessary and eventually, finding it possible to purchase the three and a half acre site in Lock's Lane, then occupied by an old laundry and a few cottages, the firm erected what was to become by the early 1950s a large modern factory, world famous for its marzipan and almond products. When, as Princess Elizabeth, the present Queen was married in 1947 Renshaws were proud to be chosen to manufacture one of her eight wedding cakes, and three years later they were granted the Royal Warrant of Approval to supply almond products to His Majesty King George VI.

By 1979, when the firm was featured in a special article in the local press, the business was in the hands of Peter and John Renshaw, grandsons of the founder. Renshaws were then employing around 400 people, and had customers throughout the bakery and retail trade ranging from corner shops to supermarkets. Overseas markets included Canada, Australia and South Africa, Denmark and the Far East. Turnover amounted to £17m. per annum, and products covered a wide range of bakery goods from ground and flaked almonds, desiccated coconut, walnuts and hazel nuts, glacé cherries and mixed peel. Finished products included cake decorations, and such delicacies as chocolate truffles and petit fours. Sadly, for after 70 years Renshaws seemed very much a permanent feature of the local scene, it was announced in 1990 that a decision had been taken by the company to close down the Mitcham factory, and to relocate production elsewhere.[4] After standing vacant for several years, the site was re-developed by Wimpey in 1995/6 as the Wordsworth Place estate of maisonette blocks.

A few further minor points of interest are perhaps worth noting before turning our attention away from Lock's Lane and Eastfields Road. In 1868 construction of the South London, Tooting and Sutton branch of the London, Brighton and South Coast Railway cut a swathe through

Mitcham, severing several farm tracks and bridleways leading from the Streatham Road to the common field and the hamlet of Lonesome, compelling all vehicular traffic and animals thereafter to converge on the new Eastfields level crossing.

By the end of the 19th century Lock's Lane, a public bridleway since time immemorial, was lit and maintained by the local highway authority, Croydon Rural District Council, as far as the bend where it is now joined by Lansdell Road. Although when laying its watermain the Council followed the lane beyond the point where the old field gate had hung, they declined to accept any responsibility for its maintenance, and the surface of the track eastwards was in an atrocious condition right across the fields as far as Lonesome Farm and Streatham Vale. In 1897, following the receipt of many petitions and individual letters of protest, together with a formal complaint from Mitcham Parish Council at the refusal of Croydon to maintain the roadway, Surrey County Council decided to hold a local public enquiry to determine responsibility for repair. At the enquiry, which was held at the Vestry Hall in May 1897, numerous witnesses were called to substantiate the case that for as long as it could be remembered, the lane between Figges Marsh and Lonesome had been in use as a public highway, with no-one being denied passage. The witnesses also gave evidence of the appalling state of the lane, which became rutted to a depth of 12 inches in winter and thick with mud, rendering it extremely unpleasant and even dangerous to women and children. The evidence makes fascinating reading, many of the witnesses being old men who could recall their youth working in the unfenced open fields, ploughing and tending the crops.[5]

Opposite today's Eastfields allotments is the 1950s housing estate of Roper Way, Ormerod Gardens etc., built on the site of a late 19th-century gravel pit, backfilled with rubbish in the inter-war years and used, after levelling and the erection of stands for spectators, as the Mitcham Stadium. In the 1930s and for a number of years after the end of World War II this was a popular venue not only for sports events, but also for carnivals, firework displays and fêtes of all kinds. The houses in Rialto Road, between the stadium and the railway line, were erected in the 1930s after the clearance of a piggery and a dilapidated terrace of 19th-century labourers' cottages. Another gravel pit, and a further row of workers' dwellings, stood near the crossing, and are now the site of the cottages forming part of Mitcham Borough Council's Laburnum Estate, built in the 1950s.

The Willows and Manor Cottage

James Drewett recalled that in the 1860s "a large house called The Willows, occupied by a Mr Taylor, stood next to The Chestnuts, overlooking Figges Marsh."[1] Like many similar houses in the village at that time, "it had extensive stabling, farmery, meadows and gardens", and in many respects would have been self-supporting. Taylor (he was a wine merchant) and his wife could afford to live in modest style, and employed a living-in cook and groom.[2]

Mitcham was about to change, however, and within 30 years The Willows had been demolished and its grounds were cleared to provide land for the estate of houses now comprising Graham Avenue, and Graham, Elmfield and Fernlea Roads. No photographs of The Willows are known, but from the outlines shown on the 1847 tithe map and the 25 inch to the mile Ordnance Map of 1865 one can see its plan was irregular, suggesting that it had been extended at various times. The site occupied was approximately that of No. 2 Graham Avenue and Nos. 17 and 19 Streatham Road. A large rectangular pond, on which Drewett remembered a boat being kept, is marked on the maps abutting the highway between The Willows and the boundary of The Chestnuts next door. This had probably originated many years before the houses were built as a pit dug in the roadside waste to obtain gravel needed for highway repairs. On the far side of The Willows were the stables, yard and outbuildings forming the 'farmery' and to the rear, beyond the formal gardens, were various enclosures, probably kept as permanent pasture for the family's horses.

The Taylors could not have lived at The Willows very long, for on the evidence of local directories a Frederick Maynard was in residence in the late 1860s.[3] Both, we can assume on the basis of the tithe survey, held the property on a lease from Samuel Oxtoby, the owner.[4] The previous occupiers had been the Milnes family, William Milnes, a coal factor, having moved from Lambeth to Mitcham with his wife and family around 1840. His was a large household – there were six daughters and two sons – and Milnes was obviously prospering, for he could afford a governess and nurse for the children, as well as a cook and houseservant.[5]

The lack of illustrations is frustrating, but parts of The Willows could well have dated from the early 18th century, if not before, for Rocque shows a building on the site.[6] Since it was the property of Oxtoby, the earlier house may have been extended around the same time as The Chestnuts, with the firm of Samuel Oxtoby and Sons being responsible for the development.

Frederick Maynard, who was described as a "Public Accountant" by the enumerator, is listed with his wife, children and servants in the returns for 1871 and 1881. He was still resident at The Willows in 1882,[7] and the family were probably the last occupants of the house, for in August 1887, described as an "old-fashioned family residence and grounds" (they actually covered a little over six acres), the property was offered for sale by auction, together with several plots of building land.[8] The map accompanying the sale particulars shows that the grounds still extended between Graham Road and Graham Avenue, with a frontage on Streatham Road. Nineteen houses had already been erected in Graham Road and Graham Avenue by this time, and judging by the style of No. 2 Graham Avenue, which now stands roughly on the site of The Willows, the old house was demolished soon after the sale.[9]

Many of the houses now occupying the land formerly covered by The Willows' grounds must, in fact, have been erected soon after the auction. Others date from the 1920s and '30s. As might be expected, they show considerable variation in size and style, although none is particularly large, and the indications are that the land was developed piecemeal by a number of different builders. Research into the plans deposited in the former Borough Surveyor's office would have enabled a more complete picture to have been drawn had the records not been destroyed in the 1970s.

Close by The Willows, Manor Cottage, a deceptively named house (for it was by no means small), stood at the corner of Sandy Lane and Streatham Road in nearly three acres of ground.[4] It was there in the 1820s, and is marked prominently on Smith's map of Surrey,[10] but its early history is not known. The tithe register shows that in the 1840s Manor Cottage was occupied by a Richard Swift, renting or leasing from Bridget Feltham, a local landowner after whom a road in the neighbourhood is named. As Drewett remembered, with the house went a large garden, outbuildings and meadow and Manor Cottage presumably ranked amongst the more noteworthy residences in this part of the parish. Richard Swift is not mentioned in the local directories of 1845 or 1851, and nothing more is known of him. The property merits a mention in this account mainly for Drewett's comment that "At the corner of Streatham Lane stood a house occupied by Mr Hurst (Hurst and Blackett) with a fine garden and meadow".[1] Daniel Hurst finds a place in the local directory of 1869, and was described in the 1871 census as a "publisher", with a business address in Great

Marlborough Street. The firm of Hurst and Blackett, of which presumably Daniel Hurst was the senior partner, was well-known before and after World War I as publishers of novels and romances. The firm no longer exists, having merged with Hutchinson and Co. Ltd, in the 1930s.

Streatham Lane, c.1910, looking north from Figges Marsh

Chapter 7

BIGGIN FARM AND GORRINGE PARK

The Tudor and Stuart Periods

Other than what we have outlined in earlier chapters, until the mid-16th century nothing much can be said of the history of Biggin Farm and the three crofts comprising the holding of Tamworth. The court rolls of Biggin from 1482 are, as we have noted, available for study. and a future researcher with a knowledge of medieval Latin may be able to uncover more details.[1] Although the last remnants of the old farmland disappeared under housing estates 70 years ago, the names and pattern of the fields surrounding Biggin in the 19th century are preserved in sale particulars from the 1820s, and also in the tithe and early Ordnance Survey maps. There are, therefore, a number of clues as to their beginnings.

Firstly, there is nothing to suggest that any of the land had been in strip holdings or part of a medieval field system. This is not altogether surprising for, compared with the fertile loams which were such a feature of the common fields lying either side of the village centre, the land in this part of Mitcham is relatively poor and, where the clay is near the surface, more difficult to work.[2] We have already suggested that it probably retained a semi-natural cover of mixed deciduous woodland into the later Middle Ages, and this supposition is supported by the predominantly rectangular pattern of the fields and meadows to be seen surrounding the farmstead in 19th-century maps. These are typical of enclosures and crofts created by the process of woodland clearance, or "assarting", a practice commonly followed as the population increased during the medieval and Tudor periods and more land needed to be brought under cultivation. Field names like Eight Acres, Pig Meadow, Pond Field, and Holly Bush Field, in use in the 19th century, prosaic in the extreme, contain none of those picturesque elements which often betray origins early in the history of a community.

Robert Wilford, to whom, as we have seen, Biggin was granted by Henry VIII in 1544 as part of the manor of Biggin and Tamworth,[3] lived in a large house in Lower Mitcham to the south of the Cricket Green. The first detailed information about the farm and its occupants in the years that followed comes from the Mitcham parish registers and contemporary wills, researched by Robert Garraway Rice in the 1870s.[4] Rice found that in a will, dated 20 February 1575,[5] "John Pyke of Bygginge in the Parisshe of Mycham ... yeoman" commended his soul to Almighty God, and directed that his body should be buried in the parish church. He bequeathed the lease of his "mansion house" of Bygginge (*sic*) with all the lands and tenements belonging thereunto to his wife Barbara for 14 years and then to his son Nicholas, she to live in the house as long as she did not remarry. If she did, the property was to be hers for eight years instead of 14.

The reference to the "mansion house" of Biggin is interesting but possibly misleading, for the Pykes' residence, although the principal dwelling on the estate, was probably little more than a substantial farmhouse. It was evidently held on a lease, and from the descent of the manor we can deduce that, if the property had not already been 'farmed' by the priory before the Dissolution, tenure was granted to Pyke either by Wilford himself, or his wife Joan, soon after his death.

"For his better helpe" Pike's son Nicholas was to have on his coming into the farm

> "one carved bedstede of Walnuttre with the whole furniture of the same belonginge and used, viz one bolster one pillowe one paire of sheetes price twentie shillings, two blanketts, one covlett, one fether bed and one mattryce".

In addition he was to receive three kine, two sows, three yearling hogs, the best brass pot, the best brass pan and the cauldron which stood "in the furnace". On his father's death Nicholas also became the owner of

> "one new longe Carte, a paire of newe wheeles shodde wit iron, Yokes and Chaines for teme oxen, one plowe and two paires of harrowes tyned with iron, ... tenne quarters of rye, three quarters of wheate, of barley fure quarters, otes five quarters, of Tares halfe a quarter, of peas half a quarter, or beans half a quarter".

John Pyke's five daughters were each to receive a legacy of £20 when attaining the age of 21, or on becoming married.

The Pyke family had been parishioners of some standing in Mitcham since the middle of the 16th century. Records show that Henry, father of John Pyke of Biggin, had been busily purchasing houses and land in Surrey since the latter part of Henry VIII's reign, but the actual source of his wealth is not known. In 1543 he bought two houses and 85 acres in Carshalton and Sutton, and in 1544 another house with land in Peckham and Camberwell. In 1550 he acquired for £40 some 11 acres in Mitcham from John and Joan Curtys who, two years before, had sold a small parcel of land in Mitcham to Sir John Mordaunt.[6] Finally, Henry Pyke added to his estate a further house with barn and land in Carshalton and Sutton, which he purchased in 1557.

Henry Pyke was a sidesman at Mitcham parish church in the reign of Edward VI.[7] The date of his death has not been verified, but it was probably around 1560, for in 1563 Elyn Pyke "widow of Henry Pyke of Byggyng" made over the property to their son John.[8] The estate which Henry assembled may have remained more or less intact for some 200 years, for the lands purchased with the Biggin property in the mid-18th century by John Manship also extended into Sutton.

At the time of his death John Pyke was holding Biggin as the lessee of Robert Wilford's widow Joan, who had remarried, becoming Lady Mordaunt of Drayton. The records of the Surrey and Kent Sewer Commission from 1569 to 1579 show that Pyke also rented, or held on sub-lease, lands bordering the Graveney owned by, or leased to, Lady Mordaunt's son-in-law Henry Whitney, serjeant to Sir Thomas Bromley the Lord Chancellor, as well as other riverside land in the tenure of Sir Gregory Lovell of Merton Abbey. The memory of one of these fields, Fleming Meade, lying between what are now Robinson and Longley Roads, is preserved today in the name of a road on the housing estate to the south, erected by Mitcham Corporation.[9]

As her late husband seems to have anticipated, Barbara Pyke remarried, taking as her second spouse Edward Russell, a member of another family owning land in Mitcham.[4] Russell held the position of "cartaker" to her majesty Queen Elizabeth, a minor office in the royal household carrying with it a modest salary. A valuation of his personal goods at the time of his death in or about 1593 shows him to have been one of the more wealthy residents in the parish but, perhaps significantly, the assessment makes no mention of lands.[10] From this we may deduce that his wife Barbara still retained title to the Biggin estate. Where Edward Russell lived is not known, but it was presumably at the Pykes' 'mansion house' at Biggin.

Nicholas Pyke predeceased his stepfather in 1591, and in the absence of any mention of the Pyke family in the tax assessments for 1593–4 we have to assume that there were no descendants on the male side. Nicholas was, however, survived by at least one sister, for in 1598 Barbara Pyke, described as one of the daughters of John Pyke of Biggin, acting with Edward Bellingham of Puttenheath, made over their interest in the manor and farm called Biggin and Tamworth to Edward Russell.[11]

Ownership of the house at Biggin is well documented, if somewhat complex, over the next 80 years. With the lordship of the manor it had become the property of Sir Nicholas Carew in 1614, and deeds dated 1635[12] and 1649[13] mention what was usually styled the "capital messuage or manor house of Biggin and Tamworth" with its barns, stables, gardens etc. and numerous parcels of land in Mitcham. The property was used as security for loans made to Sir Nicholas's son Francis by Thomas Coppin of Battersea, and title remained in the ownership of the family after Sir Francis's death in 1649[14] with the loan still outstanding. In 1654/5, following a declaration of trust and the customary procedures of lease and release, title was transferred by Carew's widow Mary via Coppin "formerly of Battersea" to George Evelyn of Wotton. This was succeeded in 1655 and 1656 by the transfer of the lordship of the manor of Biggin and Tamworth and other lands in Mitcham to Edward Thurland of the Inner Temple. Lady Carew thereby secured for herself an annuity.[15] In October 1680 George Evelyn sold to Sir Edward Thurland of Reigate "all that capital messuage or manor house of Biggin and Tamworth" plus lands as detailed in a series of deeds dating back to February 1608/9.[16] Ownership of the Mitcham house and its estate passed to Edward Thurland in 1688 on the death of his father Sir Edward, and it remained in his possession until about 1743, when it was purchased by John Manship.

In 1664 a "Gerrard Russell Esq.", the occupier, was taxed on a house in Mitcham with eight hearths.[17] Although the history of Edward Russell's family during the early part of the 17th century has not been ascertained, and locating individual houses from the 1664 tax records is somewhat imprecise, it seems not unreasonable to suggest on the evidence that the Russells remained in residence at Biggin for well over half a century. Certainly they cannot be associated with any other property in Mitcham, and actual or likely occupants for most of the larger houses in the parish can be identified with a reasonable degree of assurance.

The 18th Century

The history of the mansion house of Biggin through the early 18th century remains to be clarified, but we can assume that, if not owner-occupied, the property in all probability continued to be occupied by lessees or tenants of the Thurlands until the 1740s. A "Plan of the Farms and Lands in Mitcham being the Estate of John Manship, Lord of the Manor of Biggin and Tamworth" prepared in 1743 is obviously contemporary with the change in ownership of the property to which we have referred in the previous section.[18] It shows a group of buildings, surrounded by fields, lying between Streatham Lane and the London Road. Roughly occupying the site of the "Tamworth House" indicated on maps accompanying sale particulars 80 years later,[19] the foundations of these buildings now lie below the footings and gardens of Nos. 120–134 and 111–123 Gorringe Park Avenue.

The old Elizabethan mansion house of "Bygginge", known so well by the Pike family, was probably somewhat dilapidated by the 1740s if, in fact, it had survived the intervening centuries. As has been suggested, the term "mansion" may convey the wrong impression, and Bygginge is more likely to have remained at heart a substantial farmhouse, perhaps with some 17th-century extensions, rather than evolved into anything more imposing.

John Manship had been living at the Parsonage House, or The Canons, in Lower Mitcham since 1737, having purchased the remaining portion of the lease from the previous occupier. In 1741 he negotiated a new seven-year lease from the owner, James Cranmer,[20] but within two years purchased the Thurland estate in Mitcham, which included Biggin Farm and the manor of Biggin and Tamworth, as well as various houses and land elsewhere in the parish and over the border in Sutton. The newly acquired property seems not to have included a house suitable for the Manship household's occupation, and it may have been the intention eventually to build a new house at Biggin. This did not come about, and John Manship remained at The Canons until his death in February 1749. In his will he devised his estate to his wife Elizabeth for her life, and thereafter to his only son John.[21] Elizabeth Manship only stayed at the Canons for a short while after her husband's death, paying the last instalment of the annual ground rent due to James Cranmer in 1750.[22]

In 1748 the Manships' son John had married Ann, the daughter and heir of Richard Dowdeswell. Their only child, also named Ann, married Simon Ewart whose father, John Ewart, a London distiller, built Morden Park House in 1768.[23] A change in name from Biggin Farm to Biggin Grove between the drafting of Rocque's maps of 1741–5 and the 1760s may reflect changes taking place at this time, possibly the erection of a house more in keeping with the aspirations of a young city merchant and his new wife. However, the earliest poor rate books still extant for the parish destroy any idea that Biggin Grove was for long the Manships' home, for they show that by 1755 the house and farm, as two separate properties, were leased to Robert Beaverstock and a Mr Le Blanc.[24]

In about 1760 Biggin Grove was leased to Captain Edward Matthew(s), to whom we shall return later. This lease was surrendered around 1787, and records for the following year show Edward Evanson as the first of a succession of tenants, about whom nothing is known at the present time.[25] John Manship's name replaces that of his mother as the "proprietor" of the property in the land tax books from 1789 onwards,[26] and that year Edwards, the topographical writer, described it as "a seat belonging to John Manship Esq., one of the Directors of the East India Company."[27] "Bigging Grove", he informed his readers, was "a good house, but rather low". He did, however, take the trouble to note for posterity that "the front is towards the south-east, and opened to a road by a grass plat which is bounded by a shrubbery to the north". This lawn remained a feature of the property for many years, finding mention in the sale particulars of 1822 and in the tithe register of 1846. A quarter of a mile to the west, on the far side of Figges Marsh, ran the new turnpike road to London, from which the house was clearly visible through the trees.

John Manship junior at this time was living in Bysshe Court, near Smallfield in Surrey, and his interest in Biggin Grove could have been little more than as an investment.[28] Frequent changes in the tax assessments and description of the property which ensued over the next 20 years – for two successive years it was even valued as four separately occupied houses, each with its own land – are a sure indication of its general decline in attractiveness as a gentleman's residence.

Biggin Grove and the Matthews

On being leased by Elizabeth Manship to Captain Edward Matthew in about 1760, Biggin Grove and Mitcham acquired a new and interesting resident who, although his career took him away from the village for long periods, must have awakened local curiosity.

Edward Matthew had commenced service in the army as an ensign in the 2nd Foot Guards (The Coldstream) in 1745, and rose to become colonel of the 62nd Regiment of Foot from 1779 until 1805. His distinguished career has been outlined by Colonel Kenrick in *The Story of the Wiltshire Regiment*:

> "Thirteen years later he accompanied the Expedition to Cherbourg and St. Malo, and became a Captain and Lieutenant-Colonel in 1761. A full Colonel in 1775, he commanded the Brigade of Guards as a Brigadier in North America. The year he became Colonel of the 62nd. he was a Lieutenant-Colonel in the Guards and a Major-General in the Army. About 1784 he was Governor of Grenada, and was Commander-in-Chief in the West Indies for many years. Promoted General in 1797, he died at Glenville Lodge in Hampshire in his 78th year."[29]

General Matthew relinquished his lease of Biggin Grove in about 1787. Whilst residing in Mitcham he seems to have been accompanied by his family, one of whom, James Tilly Matthew, presumably a son, is the main subject of the following note, kindly contributed by Dr Robert J. M. V. Howard, when Registrar in Psychiatry at the Maudsley Hospital.[30]

In the 1780s James Tilly Matthew of Biggin Grove Mitcham and Camberwell, was a successful tea broker with an address at 84 Leadenhall Street in the City. In 1792 he followed the radical intellectual cleric David Williams to Paris quite uninvited. Williams was involved in secret peace negotiations between London and France which he abandoned in August 1793. Matthew, without any official backing then made a series of three "peace missions" which the French took extremely seriously, and he almost succeeded in his bizarre self-financed and self-appointed mission. The Revolutionary government were suspicious of him, however, and he was imprisoned by them 1793–6. They declared him a "dangerous Lunatic", and he made his way home to England. On arriving in London, he burst into the House of Commons in September 1796, shouted "treason!" and accused all the MPs of "traitorous venality". He was arrested and committed to Bethlem Hospital. While a patient he explained his complicated paranoid delusional system to the medical staff – he believed that a magnet had been placed in the centre of his brain, which allowed him to communicate with a group of what he called "pneumatic chemists" who operated a fearsome machine called the "air-loom" which could, by mesmeric forces, control his mind and allow him telepathic communication with the group members. There was a widespread plot, he believed, by which all the MPs and officers in the forces were similarly controlled so that the French could invade England without using any force.

James Matthew's case became a public sensation in the early 1800s and his family engaged in constant legal battles with the hospital to obtain his release. He was to die in a private madhouse in 1815 after spending 17 years confined at Bethlem, during which time he learnt engraving and published a book in 1812 called *Useful Architecture*.[31]

A book about James Matthew, entitled *Illustrations of Madness*, was published in 1810 by John Haslam. the hospital apothecary, and represents the first book-length psychiatric case history published.[30]

Lord Redesdale and Tamworth House

In 1803–4 Biggin Grove and the rest of the estate was sold by Manship or his executors, and yet another era commenced in the history of north Mitcham.

The new owner of the property was no less a person than the Rt. Hon. Lord Redesdale, newly created Lord Chancellor of Ireland and former Speaker of the House of Commons. For three years or more Lord Redesdale continued to lease the property to tenants, now re-assessed for tax purposes as comprising one fairly substantial house worth £70 per annum, and a new farmhouse which, with a little over 200 acres of land, brought in a rental of £150 per annum. Then, in 1807, the house having been vacated by a G. Dorrier Esq., its occupant since 1805, Lord Redesdale embarked upon a programme of modernisation and refurbishment which included the erection of a large new two-storeyed addition. The farm continued meantime as a separate unit, in the hands of various tenants, the last to be recorded in Mitcham poor rate books being William Lushington, to whom the premises were let by Lord Redesdale in 1811. The following year he had gone.

Before considering the work carried out at Biggin Grove under Lord Redesdale's direction we ought, perhaps, to consider briefly the man and his career. John Freeman Mitford, the first baron Redesdale, was born in Holborn in 1748. Educated initially at Cheam School, he was called to the bar in 1777, and rapidly acquired a large practice, having achieved considerable fame through a treatise on pleadings in Chancery. He was returned as Member of Parliament for Bere Alston, Devonshire, in 1788, and became a King's Counsel in the following year. On 11 February 1801 he was elected Speaker of the House of Commons, and a year later was created Baron Redesdale and was appointed Lord Chancellor of Ireland. He died in 1830 at Batsford Park, near Moreton-in-Marsh, Gloucestershire. Lord Redesdale was described by a contemporary as a "sallow man, with round face and blunt features, of a middle height, thickly and heavily built", with "a heavy, drawling tedious manner of speech". He was also said to have been completely lacking any sense of humour.[32] Redesdale married Lady Frances

Mitcham

Biggen & Tamworth. Baron Redesdale. pulled down

Perceval in 1803, and it may well have been under her guiding influence that he set about transforming his property at Mitcham.

An increase in the assessed value of the estate from £220 p.a. in 1807 to £386 in 1812 and £428 in 1820 can be taken as an indication of the scale of the works carried out under Lord Redesdale's direction. A sketch of the new south-eastern elevation of the house, dated 1826, shortly after it was demolished, depicts a two-storeyed building in the style of, but very much smaller than, Henry Holland's 'marine villa' of 1787 at Brighton for the Prince of Wales.[33] A plan of Redesdale's estate dated 1818 shows the new wing extending across the whole of the south-east frontage of the earlier house, overlooking the lawn.[34] This again echoes the approach adopted at Brighton where part of the original 'Georgian' farmhouse was retained within the new Royal Pavilion . Although the scale of the plan is rather small, it can be seen that at Mitcham the older building backing the modest new wing was U-shaped in plan and faced north-west.

Tamworth House, as the enlarged and modernised Biggin Grove was renamed by the Redesdales, together with the farm and land, was offered for sale by auction at Garraways Coffee House, Cornhill, on 26 March 1818.[34] The "desirable family residence improved at considerable expense with offices of all description, coach houses and stables" was accompanied by a "newly-built farm house, with gardens, barns, stables, outbuildings and sundry enclosures of meadow, pasture and arable land in a high state of cultivation, all lying compact, bounded by a stream of water" (i.e. the Graveney on the north) "and the roads from Tooting and Streatham to Mitcham". Perhaps a sign that Mitcham was passing out of fashion as a location for country retreats, the notice of sale goes on to emphasise the abundance on the property of "very fine gravel, which would be an almost inexhaustible source of wealth to a purchaser". The attached plan shows the estate extending some 25 chains (500m) eastwards, beyond the road to Streatham and bounded on the south by the Little Graveney, flowing from the direction of Pollards Hill. Beyond this watercourse lay land owned by James Moore, and now the site of Gorringe Park School.

Within Tamworth House were

"On the Chamber Storey, two spacious bed chambers, and two dressing rooms overlooking the lawn, neatly finished marble chimney pieces, handsome paper etc; eight other bed chambers, and a dressing room; a roomy open Vestibule between the chambers; water closet, etc., principal and secondary staircases ..."

on the ground floor there was a

" ... spacious entrance hall, and water closet; a vestibule leading to a capital lofty drawing room, handsomely papered, enriched cornices, marble chimney-piece, and window to the lawn; a dining parlour of the same proportions, with marble chimney piece etc., and a library, also with a marble chimney piece."

The domestic quarters, probably in the rear, and older part, of the house, were extensive, but typical of a gentleman's house of the period:

"A housekeeper's room, fitted with dressers, presses and shelves; a butler's pantry, with dressers, shelves etc., servants' hall, paved with stone, and bed room adjoining; an excellent kitchen, fitted with dresser, shelves etc., ... A scullery, with pump of good water; larder etc., dry and convenient cellars."

An enclosed yard contained

" ... a dairy, a wood and coal house, knife house, and a pump of good water, sink etc., a wash house and laundry over, with shelves etc. Gardeners' room, loft etc. A four-stall stable, two coach-houses, and lofts etc. A kitchen garden, paled round, and planted with fruit trees; a smaller kitchen garden; open lawn, surrounded by pleasure grounds and plantations, ornamented with fine-grown Timber Trees and Shrubs."

The principal part of Tamworth House, "a capital family residence, seated on a lawn, enclosed from the road by a paling etc." was stated to have been erected only a few years previously. Biggin Farm House, "a compact brick-built dwelling, convertible at a small expense into a cottage ornée" was offered for sale at the same time with some 29 acres of meadow and arable land.

Whilst Lord Redesdale was still in possession of the estate, C. and R. Greenwood visited Tamworth House and described it as an "elegant and ancient mansion with extensive and beautiful grounds and plantations" – a description which seems fully justified by the impression given by the sale particulars and supports the belief that in part it was the Elizabethan house of the Pykes.[35] Redesdale's decision to sell so soon after creating what clearly was a most attractive and desirable house at the heart of a modest country estate – ideal, one would have thought, for someone with business in London – is therefore at first sight surprising. The explanation almost certainly lies in his bereavement in August 1817, when his wife died at their house in Harley Street, London. To compound Lord Redesdale's misfortune, his attempt to find a buyer coincided with a period of acute economic recession following the end of the Napoleonic Wars. At this time profits to be derived from land and other forms of investment were declining sharply, and many of the gentry were brought to near ruin. Symptomatic of the prevailing climate was the absence of any acceptable offer for Tamworth House and Biggin Farm, and the property was withdrawn from sale.

Four years later, perhaps pressed for money himself, Lord Redesdale again placed the property on the market. This time, however, he was evidently determined to cut his losses and to salvage what he could. Tamworth House had already been demolished, and the building materials were listed as a separate item in the catalogue. The site of the house was offered as one lot with its coach house, outbuildings and garden still intact. The virtues of the newly-built farmhouse, "conveniently planned and adapted for the Accommodation of a respectable Family" were repeated and, as at the earlier auction, the potential value of the gravel, excavation of which would have ruined parts of the estate for ever, was not overlooked in the effort to attract a purchaser.[36]

Gorringe Park House, and William and Fanny Harris

The sale of Lord Redesdale's Mitcham estate in 1822, in so far as it secured a buyer for Biggin Farm, can be said to have been successful, but Tamworth House was no more, and its stables, outbuildings and rickyard became part of the farmstead.[37] The new owner, William Fuller, was a working farmer, who continued for some 25 years without, so far as is known, playing any outstanding role in the affairs of the parish.[38] He may have been the father of another William Fuller, who was growing medicinal and aromatic herbs at Carshalton later in the 19th century, but other than that, all we can say about him was that when the tithe commutation survey was conducted in Mitcham in 1846 Fuller had 183 acres of land either side of Streatham Lane, 110 of which were arable and 52 kept either as meadow or rough pasture.[39] The remainder was taken up by the house, gardens, shrubberies etc.

The census return for 1851 shows Biggin Farm providing employment for 15 labourers, but the owners, who were absent when the census was conducted, were not named. The Post Office *Directory* for 1851, however, lists them as John and Isaac Rutter and Co., the snuff and tobacco manufacturers, whose mills were on the Wandle at Ravensbury. Traditional mixed farming seems to have been in general decline in the neighbourhood of Mitcham by the mid-19th century, and this is probably reflected in repeated changes at Biggin in the 1850s and '60s. In 1855, according to a later edition of the same directory, the farm was in the hands of Samuel Rust, but in 1862 Jacob Maas, "farmer" is listed at "Biggin Stud Farm". Maas, aged 46 and a native of Hesse-Darmstadt, with his British-born wife Mary Ann, were listed in the Census in 1861. Despite the advent of the railways, road transport at this time relied almost exclusively on horses, and the demand for animals both as mounts and for the drawing of vehicles remained virtually insatiable. A major part of the economy of villages around the capital was directed towards meeting the requirements of this market, be it in raising and training of horses, the production of hay and forage, or the construction and repair of vehicles. In this context it is not surprising to find the census enumerator in 1861 noting that Maas had ten men and two boys employed whole time about the business of the stud farm. The household at Biggin gave further employment, and a governess was engaged to care for the four Maas children, whilst there were also three domestic servants living-in.

The Ordnance Survey map of 1865 confirms the farm still to be in existence three years later, the outline of the buildings little altered since 1822. Change was in the air once more, however, and the farmhouse was soon to disappear to make way for the building of Gorringe Park House, a substantial, three-storeyed three-bay brick and slate-roofed mansion in the modified version of the Italianate style which had become popular in the 1850s. The farmyard, complete with its piggeries, rickyard and barns, was retained, but the meadows and orchards in the immediate vicinity of the house were transformed to form gardens and parkland. The old farm lane became a long, winding entrance drive, with lodges and gates where Bruce Road now meets Gorringe Park Avenue, and at the junction of St James's Road with Streatham Road.

William John Harris, for whom the new house seems to have been built, was born in about 1803 at Southwark, and his wife Fanny around 1809 at Ringmer in Sussex. In the census of 1871 William Harris's "occupation" was given as "Landed Proprietor", but a decade later the enumerator was a little more specific, and described the source of his income as being "land, house property and Government Annuities". Of the source of this wealth and his antecedents we know nothing for certain, but William Harris seems to have been related to the Moore family through his grandmother, Maria Louisa, who was James Moore's sister and married Captain Edward Kelly of the Light Dragoons in 1796. Kelly served with the Life Guards at Waterloo, where he acquitted himself with distinction and was severely wounded. He died in 1828 in India, whilst Lieutenant-Colonel of the 59th Native Infantry.[40] One of his seven daughters, Harriet St Clair Kelly, married Francis Harris M.D., son of Robert Harris, for many years Deputy Lieutenant and a magistrate of Surrey. A large marble tablet to their memory can be seen in the north transept of Mitcham parish church, which was owned by Harriet's uncle, James Moore.

The erection of Gorringe Park House and the conversion of Biggin Farm into a park can be dated to the period between 1865 and 1871, when the Harrises took up residence. The establishment recorded in the census speaks of affluence, for William and Fanny, both then in their sixties, employed a living-in staff of butler, cook, housemaids and groom. The remainder of the farm outbuildings had been refurbished to become what the enumerator called "Gorringe Park Stables", in which

Gorringe Park House, Mitcham (© P J Loobey 2001)

The Avenue, Gorringe Park, Mitcham (© P J Loobey 2001)

there was accommodation for Henry Fillmore, the Harrises' coachman, Mrs Fillmore and their two sons, one of whom was employed as a blacksmith. In the newly-built lodges at the ends of the drive lived two more families, one headed by a carpenter and the other the estate gardener.

The Harrises were childless, as far as we can ascertain, and, with their daily needs and the maintenance of the estate in the hands of staff, their lives seem to have been centred very much on the new church and parish of Christ Church, Colliers Wood. Their main claim to a place in local history, in fact, rests securely in the part they played in establishing this parish, formed in 1875 by the severance of North Mitcham and Colliers Wood from the rest of the ancient ecclesiastical parish of Mitcham.

As a temporary measure, a mission room had been opened in Merton Road (now Christchurch Road) in 1864. This was enlarged three years later, but it was recognised that the rapidly expanding suburb of Colliers Wood, or "Merton Singlegate", as it was often known, deserved better provision. William Harris's name was already familiar on lists of subscribers to parish charities when, in 1871, it was announced that a contribution of £2,500 by Mr and Mrs Harris had made possible the erection of a fine new church – Christ Church – in the lane leading from Colliers Wood to Mitcham. One of the foundation stones was laid in June 1873 by William Harris, and he and his wife appointed the first vicar, the Revd Henry Barber of Tulse Hill. The new parish was formed in August 1875 and boundary stones were set in place the same year. One of them, at the roadside in Streatham Road opposite the lodge of Gorringe Park House, remained in place until 1968, when it was transferred at the writer's suggestion to the grounds of Christ Church for safe keeping.

Patronage of the living at Christ Church was vested by deed in William and Fanny Harris until their deaths,[41] and in 1882 notice of their benefaction of £5,000 to secure a stipend for the incumbent was published in the *London Gazette*. In 1884 the Harrises presented Christ Church with a peal of six bells and a brass lectern, and their generosity continued until William Harris's death in December 1894 at the age of

91. His wife, who was six years his junior, died in May 1898. Their passing was sincerely mourned by their fellow parishioners. A stained glass window, installed in 1895 to the memory of William Harris, was destroyed by German bombing during the 1939–45 war, but a simple brass tablet to the patrons' memory can still be seen in the chancel at Christ Church. Fanny Harris is also commemorated by a marble memorial, and the "Fanny Harris Charity", which she endowed with £500, is devoted to providing annual Sunday School prizes.

Gorringe Park – The Last Years

Soon after the deaths of the Harrises, Gorringe Park House was acquired by the Barbican Mission to the Jews, in whose hands it became a residential home for Jewish men seeking a knowledge of the Christian faith. The house also provided accommodation for the Mission's secretary and later director, Prediger Christlieb Traugott Lipshytz,[43] but it was probably best known by the residents of Mitcham in its subsequent role as the Naomi Home for Children, an orphanage for Jewish children, also under the auspices of the Barbican Mission.[43]

The development of north Mitcham by speculative builders had, of course, begun well before the end of Victoria's reign. Railway construction had already cut a swathe across the fields to the north of Biggin Farm when the Harrises came to Gorringe Park, and Tooting Station on the London, Brighton and South Coast Railway Company's line from Wimbledon was opened in 1868. But it was the extension of the tramway network along Southcroft Road and southwards to Mitcham almost 40 years later that provided the great stimulus to the expansion of the suburbs of South London, and the tree-fringed meadows of Tooting and Streatham began to disappear rapidly beneath the advance of bricks and mortar once the tramways were in operation.

In Gorringe Park Avenue, near its junction with London Road, four substantial houses – "Gorringe Park Villas" – had been built and occupied by 1881, and in the mid-1890s there were terraces of shops, flats, and houses immediately to the south of Tooting Junction station, which was opened in 1894. For a brief spell, however, the tide was partially stemmed by the links of Tooting Golf Course, which extended

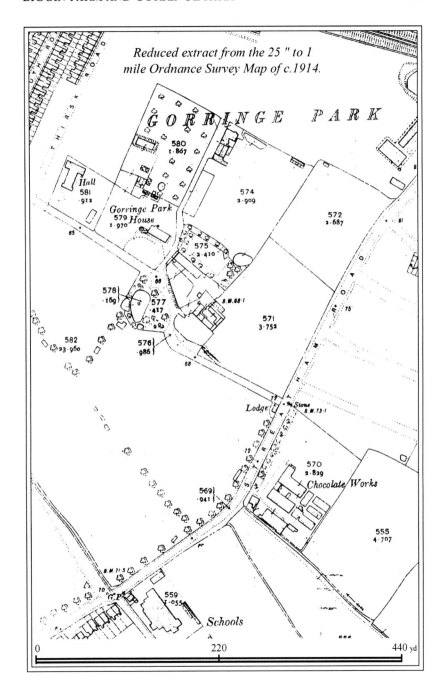

Reduced extract from the 25 " to 1
mile Ordnance Survey Map of c.1914.

eastwards from where Tooting Police Station now stands to the vicinity of Roe Bridge near Southcroft Corner. Soon after the turn of the century the Links Estate, taking its name from the golf course, was laid out by the land owner, Sir Charles Seely, between the Graveney and the railway line from Tooting Junction to Streatham Vale as far as Roe Bridge. Between Links Road and Seely Road terraces of well-built villas appeared, arranged in a street pattern reminiscent of the rungs of a ladder, and named alphabetically from Ascot and Boscombe to Ipswich and Jersey.

With the arrival of the 20th century the rate of house-building to the south of the railway gradually gained momentum, and several distinct estates were to emerge in north Mitcham, each with its own style. Early in this period three of the four new villas in Gorringe Park Avenue were demolished to provide a site for a terrace of houses. Behind these, and extending back to the Tooting Junction end of Ashbourne Road, a grid-pattern development of parallel roads with closely-packed terraces of houses and flats was well advanced by 1914.

Melrose Avenue - postcard c. 1910

On an outcrop of London Clay towards the Streatham Road end of Ashbourne Road a brickworks appeared early in the Edwardian period, its tall chimney topping the trees. Here some 20 years later, builder Joseph Owen[44] (believed to have been a great-grandson of James Moore and a distant cousin of the Harrises) was to erect the North Mitcham Improvement Association's Hall in Woodland Way to replace the ex-army hut put up as a temporary measure in 1919.[45] It was no doubt at these works that many of the bricks and tiles used in the new houses in the district were made. The large clay pit left when the works closed was eventually back-filled, but the land was unsuitable for building for many years and remained largely vacant until the late 1970s. Eventually the whole site was redeveloped, and it is now occupied by an estate of small houses begun in the 1980s.

Whilst the first phase of building in Gorringe Park was in progress, much of the parkland surrounding the Harrises' former home was let off for various leisure activities. Tooting Graveney Football Club had its pitches on part of the old farm, which Kelly's *Directory* for 1905 records as a "Home for Horses", and there were several cricket pitches. Pony racing is said to have been a regular feature, drawing large crowds, and for a number of years a corner of the park was the headquarters of a travelling fair.

The outbreak of war in 1914 was the reason for the first phase of house-building coming to an abrupt halt, and it was not until the 1920s that what remained of the Gorringe Park estate was finally broken up and building recommenced. During this prolonged transitional period, lasting almost ten years, the area was hardly attractive, although many of the park trees survived to hide the worst eyesores. Whilst the threat of demolition was temporarily suspended, little was done to maintain the old mansion and its gardens, and their condition became more and more dilapidated. Part of the park had become war-time allotments, but the house continued in use as an orphanage, and with the stables and other farm buildings remained standing until after the Armistice.

The Merchant Taylors' stone, Roe bridge (c.1970)

THE STREATHAM ROAD

Roe Bridge

The river Graveney, its name allegedly derived from the manor of Tooting Graveney through which it flowed on its way to join the Wandle below Colliers Wood, has served as a boundary between Mitcham and Streatham for a thousand years or more. It provided a convenient line of demarcation between the ecclesiastical parishes when they came into existence in the early Middle Ages, and still defines the boundary between the London Boroughs of Merton and Wandsworth.

Mitcham's Streatham Road, known until the end of the 19th century as Streatham Lane, led from one Saxon village to another and undoubtedly had its origins in a track or bridle way of considerable antiquity. A Roman road south from London passed through Streatham, and for centuries the traveller making for Mitcham would have been obliged to cross the Graveney by a ford which, unless it was paved, would have became very muddy and even dangerous during bad weather. The approaches to the river could also become hazardous, as can be judged from a minute of the Sewer Commissioners in 1572, which required "Francis Carew Esquier" to

> " ... cope and make higher than now is to ye quantity of one fote his banke against the river of Biggre (Graveney) in the parish of Micham ... with good faste and sounde earthe as welle for the kepinge in of the water as for the tramplinge of horsemen with treadinge it downe although it was latelye done conteninge by estimacion iiij roddes."[1]

Sir Francis Carew was a major landowner in Mitcham, with property which evidently extended northwards as far as the Graveney ("the river of Biggre", or Biggin). The damaged bank seems likely to have been immediately upstream from the Streatham Lane ford, since in the 1570s the land below the crossing was in the possession of John Pyke who, we have seen in an earlier chapter, held Biggin Farm as a leasehold tenant of Henry Whitney, serjeant of Sir Thomas Bromley, the Lord Chancellor.

Local tradition maintains that the first bridge over the Graveney at this point was erected by the Worshipful Company of Merchant Taylors after Thomas Roe had narrowly escaped drowning when thrown by his horse whilst crossing the river.[2] Although it appears impossible to confirm this account from the Merchant Taylors' records, research in 1992 by John Brown of the Streatham Society showed that Thomas Roe, who in later life received a knighthood at the hands of Elizabeth I, was indeed a member of the Merchant Taylors Company, of which he became Master in 1553. In 1560 Roe was appointed Sheriff of London, and in 1568 was afforded the honour of being elected Lord Mayor. Whether or not Sir Thomas was responsible for having the bridge constructed we shall probably never discover, but he was known for good works in his lifetime. He died in 1570 and is still remembered in the City for leaving money towards the support of poor members of the Merchant Taylors Company, as well as members of the Clothworkers, Armourers, Carpenters, Tilers and Plasterers Companies.[3]

Roe bridge, Streatham Road, Mitcham. The south parapet, showing the
Surrey County Council/London County Council boundary plaque. (1972)

It is not until the reign of Charles I that we have the first mention of an actual bridge over the Graveney, records of the manor of Tooting Bec containing an entry of about 1647 which appears to refer to Roe Bridge.[4] During the Commonwealth a new stone bridge was built, presumably to replace the older structure which had then fallen into decay.

Set in the northern parapet of the bridge today one can still see a block of Portland stone on which are carved the arms of the Company with the date 1652 and the words of a now barely legible inscription recording that "This bridge was made at the cost of the Worshipful Company of Merchant Taylors". This seems proof enough but, once again, the records of the Company are not particularly helpful,[2] and contain no reference to a specific payment for the building of the bridge at this time. It could well be, however, that part of the Wilford bequest, to which we will return later, was actually used for this purpose, which would certainly account for the Merchant Taylors' arms and the inscription appearing on the bridge.

The following century the Company's archives are more forthcoming. A letter from the surveyor of highways for Streatham in 1762 claimed that money for the bridge was usually paid by the Merchant Taylors once every three years, and there is a record of three years' income being paid over in 1770 as a contribution towards the complete rebuilding of the bridge with a wider carriageway.[5] On this occasion a further inscription was added, reading:

> "This Bridge Built by the Company Named on the opposite stone was taken down Rebuilt & Enlarged in 1772 By the Munificence of the Gentry In the Neighbouring Parishes in Concurrence with the said Company."

Following receipt of complaint that the 18th-century bridge was falling into disrepair, it was reconstructed by the London County Council in 1906 and the old Merchant Taylors' stone was reset in the northern parapet. Further reconstruction took place in 1911 when the roadway was widened by the London County Council and Surrey County Council acting jointly. This work was commemorated by a small stone tablet inscribed with the words "Rebuilt 1911", and inserted into the northern parapet beneath the Merchant Taylors' stone. A bronze boundary plaque in the form of a shield, embossed "Roe Bridge LCC/SCC", was also fixed on the southern parapet.

In 1992 the bridge was again rebuilt, this time by the London Borough of Wandsworth. The stone bearing the Merchant Taylors' arms, was carefully set aside and refixed during the course of work, and a new commemorative plate was unveiled with due ceremony on 10 November 1992 by Cllr Peter Donoghue, the Deputy Mayor of Wandsworth, and John R. Perring, Past Master of the Merchant Taylors Company.

John Perring unveils the new commemorative plate on 10 November 1992

A Country Lane

To a limited extent during the Middle Ages highways outside towns were maintained by the Church, but this ceased with the dissolution of the monasteries by Henry VIII between 1534 and 1539. Thereafter responsibility was occasionally assumed by individuals or guilds, and in various parts of the country there were some notable and praiseworthy improvements carried out voluntarily by local gentlemen at their own expense.

We do not know what role, if any, Merton Priory performed in maintaining the road from Biggin towards the rest of their estate over the parish border in Streatham. However, we do have in Mitcham the example of public spirit displayed by two members of the Wilford family whose connections with the parish went back to the late 15th century. The first was James Wylford *(sic)*, Master of the Worshipful Company of Merchant Taylors in 1494, who is credited with having paid for the construction of the road from Streatham to Mitcham, where he had a fine house.[1] We have also seen that by the mid-16th century the family was obviously well regarded by those in authority, and that in 1544 Robert Wilford was granted the lordship of the manor of Biggin and Tamworth and with it land in north Mitcham formerly owned by the priory. James's son John, who was Master of the Company in 1542 and owned land and a house in Lower Mitcham, followed the example set by his late father, and in his will dated 1550/51 left £13 a year, being rents from his estate, in trust to the Company to be applied to repairing the highways through Streatham, Mitcham, Carshalton and Sutton.[1] The money from the Wilford bequest was paid to the parishes of Streatham and Mitcham every three years, and for over 300 years was expended in procuring loads of stones to fill the larger holes, and buying faggots and sticks to place over the deepest mud. Eventually the costs involved in administering the annual payment from the Trust became greater than the value of the bequest. It was therefore decided, with the consent of the local authorities concerned, that payments should cease and the trust be consolidated with other charities run by the Merchant Taylors Company.[2]

Laudable as such individual gestures were, nationally such a haphazard approach to the repair of the roads fell far short of what was needed. Perhaps not unexpectedly, dissatisfaction with the condition of the main highways was widespread by the 17th century. Responsibility was placed on the parish councils by the Highways Act of 1555, but whereas they discharged their duties tolerably enough in village centres, or in the vicinity of houses owned by the more important parishioners, the condition of the roads in the more outlying parts of their districts was a constant source of complaint, particularly from those obliged to travel longer distances.

James Malcolm, describing conditions in Surrey in 1805, said of the roads in the vicinity of Mitcham

> "In following this line of road down Balam Hill, we find that in summer it is deep in dust, and in the winter deep in mud, and so it continues the whole of the way to Mitcham, insomuch that the Brighton coaches, and many of the Carshalton, Mitcham, and Sutton teams, prefer going up Mitcham-lane to Streatham, and thence along the wash-way to London, though round about, to the unpleasantness of wading through the dirt or sand of Tooting, Balam, etc.. In the first place no regard is paid to watercourses, nor to the level of the road, but it is in hills and holes, in clay or in sand all the way. Mitcham itself is always in a bad state, and never will be otherwise while those high trees are suffered to stand, which excludes both sun and air; the road is all too narrow and too low; at the entrance, and through the town of Sutton, the road is very bad, nor is it as good as it should be over Walton Heath ..."[3]

Malcolm was writing 60 years after the major routes through north-east Surrey had been turnpiked, so his strictures were aimed as much at the turnpike trustees as the parish authorities. Mitcham vestry, in many respects a model of its time, no doubt attempted to discharge its duty to the best of its abilities, but Streatham Lane (which was not turnpiked) undoubtedly had its problems. A few old photographs survive from the latter part of the 19th century, showing the trees – mostly elm – of which Malcolm complained, but whereas their removal might have helped the road to dry out, this would seem unlikely to have proved a complete solution, for the water table was normally high, and alongside the lane, roughly from the entrance to Gorringe Park as far as Sandy Lane, there flowed the Little Graveney, which at times overflowed. Beyond Gorringe Park lodge the road rose gently to breast an outcrop of London Clay, sticky in winter and deeply rutted in summer, before descending again to the valley of the Graveney.

Emma Bartley, who could remember Mitcham in the 1840s, described "Streatham Lane, from Figg's Marsh to the Parish Schools at Streatham" as "one of the most lonely roads at or near Mitcham. In the middle of the Lane there was a beer shop, but no other house".[4] Streatham Lane remained a narrow country road until the end of the 19th century and, apart from Manor Cottage and Gorringe Park lodge, there were no houses at all between Figges Marsh and the Streatham border.[5] Either side the lane was shut in with hedges or the park fence, and overhung by tall trees. At night it could be very dark and eerie, and towards the end of the 19th century the lane acquired a bad reputation. The folklore of Victorian London is rich with the alleged exploits of 'Spring-heeled Jack' who, it was commonly believed amongst the more credulous members of the population, wore 'spring-heeled boots' which enabled him to take extraordinary leaps. These, it was claimed, enabled him to appear suddenly from behind the hedgerows, startling women and young people. In his boyhood in the 1880s Tom Francis had heard it said that Streatham Lane was one of Jack's haunts, and he used to retell the tale when giving his lantern slide talks on 'Old Mitcham', but how far there was any truth in the yarn, it is impossible to say.[6]

The Impact of the Railways

It is easy for us today to overlook the dramatic effect construction of the railways during the mid-19th century could have on the old pattern of minor roads and bridle paths which for centuries had linked village centres with isolated hamlets and farmsteads. In many ways, of course, the coming of the railways was an incredible boon to our Victorian ancestors, enabling them to undertake journeys on a daily basis that had previously been rare and costly expeditions. The transport of goods was also revolutionised, and local shopkeepers were no longer reliant on village craftsmen, or what the carriers could bring on their horse-drawn wagons from far-away factories and the Thames-side docks. At times, however, the railways might actually increase the isolation of some communities by destroying, or at best diverting, old footpaths and bridle ways. In the process occupiers of outlying clusters of cottages, finding themselves separated from the villages with which they been had associated in the past, were obliged to reorientate themselves towards other centres of population. This can be demonstrated very clearly in Mitcham by citing the case of Lonesome, or 'Streatham Vale' as it came to be known.

Where main highways had to be crossed, the railway engineers had several solutions, and lowering of Streatham Lane to carry the road beneath the new bridge constructed to take the track from Tooting Junction to Streatham in 1868 presented no problem, although flooding after heavy rain could at times be dramatic. For minor roads and farm tracks less expensive solutions were sought, ranging from crossings 'on the level', either gated or ungated, to footbridges where only pedestrian traffic needed to be considered and outright closure where objectors were few or had no influence. All three were employed on the London, Brighton and South Coast Railway Company's line from Streatham to Mitcham Junction.

For that part of Mitcham close to the Streatham boundary at the end of Greyhound Lane, the construction of the railway was to have serious consequences in years to come. As the tag 'Lonesome' implies, the hamlet had long been recognised as one of the most isolated parts of the parish. In the middle of the 19th century there was, admittedly, very little there – a "Lonely House" is marked on maps of the 1820s, and 30 years later, Lonesome Farm, a few cottages and a horse slaughterhouse were all there was to be seen. The population was negligible, and as a consequence, the railway company obviously felt able to ignore them. For centuries Lonesome had been reached by way of two footpaths or bridleways leading off Streatham Lane to the north of Figges Marsh and, indirectly, via Lock's Lane and then by paths across the old common field. This orientation of Lonesome towards North Mitcham can be seen in the census records up to and including 1861, the local registrar as a matter of course including Lonesome in the enumeration district comprising that part of Upper Mitcham lying to the east of Streatham Lane.

The lanes are shown quite prominently in the earliest detailed map we have of Mitcham, produced by Edwards to illustrate his *Companion from London to Brighthelmston* first published around 1790. Edwards marked no actual buildings at Lonesome, and the remote position of the hamlet can best be appreciated from maps such as that produced by Stanford in 1862. Like the other two routes, the first and most northerly of the three, a footpath from Streatham Lane, had probably existed for many years. It gave its name to an adjacent enclosure, Green Lane Field, roughly on the site of the modern Mitcham Industrial Estate, but has now disappeared, except for a truncated length which survives as Bolstead Lane on the other side of the railway.

Sandy Lane, further to the south, remained in use after 1868, but with a crossing for pedestrians only to Grove Road. The main access to Eastfields for vehicles and farm stock was recognised as being along Lock's Lane, and here the railway company was obliged to provide a gated crossing. This has remained the situation to the present day. When house building commenced at Lonesome around the 1890s it was towards Streatham, rather than Mitcham, that the new residents turned for shopping and work.

Urbanisation

The northern end of Streatham Lane, or Streatham Road as it was shown on the 1894 O.S. Map, was the first to become developed. Here, as the end of the century approached, the old landscape of fields and country lanes was being transformed dramatically, and by the early years of the Edwardian period streets of houses already covered much of the land towards Streatham. On the Mitcham side of the Graveney the Streatham Road frontage south to the railway was largely built-up by 1914, a few shops being added near the bridge in 1921. Rustic and Rural Ways, covering the old Bridge Field and Yorkshire Field of Biggin Farm, were developed in a piecemeal fashion over a period of some 20 years, but on the opposite side of the road the Links Estate was nearing completion by 1914.

To the east of the main road and south of the railway bridge, where the terraces of houses on the Avenues Estate were to be built, any worthwhile pockets of sand and gravel which here and there capped the underlying clay were first excavated and utilised before actual house building commenced. By the outbreak of war in August 1914 the neat terraces of Park, Caithness and Melrose Avenues were completed, the roads tree-lined and with rolled gravel surfaces. Anxious to secure 'respectability' for the new neighbourhood, the estate developers stipulated that no licensed premises should be opened within one mile of the Gorringe Park Hotel – a condition which, years later, the North Mitcham Association, wishing to have a bar in its Woodland Hall, had difficulty in overcoming. Many of the breadwinners in the new households worked in Tooting or Streatham, and even central London, but travelling was easy on the new electric trams, which came as far as Southcroft Corner and offered cheap 'workmen's tickets' to those prepared to start their journeys early. A parade of excellent local shops with living accommodation above extended from Park Avenue almost as far as Melrose Avenue, but although three more roads were planned, this was as far as the new housing estate had reached by 1914, and three large fields, the former Front Meadow, Six Acres and Nine Acres of Biggin Farm, extending back from Streatham Road to the railway, marked the edge of open country until after the Armistice,

The Links Estate was already part of the Mission District of St Paul, Furzedown when, in 1903, North Mitcham was assigned by the Anglican Church to a new mission district within the parish of Christ Church Colliers Wood. At this stage, however, the Avenues Estate was so remote from Christ Church, and so difficult to reach from Mitcham that it was temporarily assigned to St James, West Streatham. A mission church was soon established in a pre-fabricated corrugated iron building in Gorringe Park, but in 1908 the foundation stone of a fine permanent church hall, designed by H. P. Burke-Downing, a local resident, was laid by H.R.H. Princess Marie Louise Augusta of Schleswig-Holstein. This building was dedicated and opened by Dr Hook, bishop of Kingston, in January 1909, after which the old mission hall was dismantled and re-erected close by for the Sunday school. The land originally occupied by the 'Iron Room' is now covered by the chancel of St Barnabas' church, a building described by Nairn and Pevsner as "big, thoughtful, neo-Bodley" and "quite sensitive".[1] Inside, the church appears vast and lacking colour, and when visited by the author in 1998 was badly in need of refurbishment. The architect was again Burke-Downing, who was one of the members of Christ Church Colliers Wood who had worked hard in the cause of the new parish. The foundation stone laid in 1913 by the Lord Mayor of London, Sir William Burnett, can be seen in the baptistry.

St Barnabas' Church,
Gorringe Park Avenue,
Mitcham (1975)

During preparation of the site for the new church what remained of Gorringe Park stables, then known as Tyrell's Farm, was demolished. A small link with this recent past was retained in the shape of a clock, removed from one of the old farm buildings and installed in the church tower through the generosity of Joseph Wilson and his wife, who around the time the church was being built were living at Gorringe Park House.

The early years of the Gorringe Park District Mission were chronicled in *The Record* and subsequently in the St Barnabas magazine. In a little booklet published in 1939 on the church's 25th anniversary, the

Revd E. J. Baker M.A., who was appointed to the mission in 1906 by the bishop of Southwark and in 1915 became the first vicar of St Barnabas', also recounted his memories of the events leading to the creation of the new parish and the consecration of the newly completed church by the bishop in November 1914. The whole story is an interesting one, and is fortunately well documented.[3] The role performed by the Church as the new community endured first the war years and then adjusted to the greatly changed circumstances of the 1920s also makes a fascinating study, but lies beyond the limits of this history.

Amongst the many who gave their support to the new Church was Joseph Wilson's brother Isaac (later Sir Isaac) Wilson. He was born in 1862, the son of a Cumbrian farmer, and although he had a successful drapery business in Durham, was persuaded to join his brothers' expanding building firm in London. For a time Isaac and his wife Sarah Ann lived at Fulham and then, in the early 1900s, they moved to No. 2 Gorringe Park Avenue where Isaac, described as a 'builder', was listed in Kelly's *Directories* for 1907 to 1913. Whilst living in north Mitcham the Wilsons became active members of St Barnabas' Church, where Isaac Wilson was a churchwarden for a number of years. Many of the houses in the vicinity of Gorringe Park Avenue were built by the Wilsons' firm, and Isaac amassed a respectable fortune, a large part of which he was to devote to the building of Mitcham Garden Village for the elderly and infirm, and the Wilson Hospital.

The political story of North Mitcham ward, which evolved in parallel with that of the Church during the inter-war years is equally interesting, and can be followed in the local press, the minutes of the Urban District Council and the *North Mitcham Sentinel,* copies of which can be consulted in the Local Studies Centre at Morden.

The first large-scale intrusion of industry into north Mitcham had its origin in a serious fire which, in October 1897, devasted the Blackfriars factory and warehouse of James Pascall, the Croydon baker's son whose sugar confectionery had already earned a world-wide reputation. Temporary premises acquired in Blackfriars after the fire enabled production to continue, but the steady expansion of the firm, which at about this time became a limited company, made it imperative that a site for a new factory should be found, away from the dirt and congestion of inner London. In north Mitcham, which offered the ideal location, land was available. Following the death of James Bridger, the Manor Farm estate was broken up and sold in 1888.[4] Lot 13, a two and three-quarter acre field abutting Streatham Lane to the north of Sandy Lane remained undeveloped for nine years, and it was here, soon after the turn of the century, that Pascall's new chocolate factory, the 'Furzedown Works', arose. Relocation to Mitcham, and the move to the spacious and modern factory on the edge of the country, was always regarded as a milestone in the evolution of the firm that had started in a little shop off Oxford Street in 1866.[5] Transfer of the company's production and warehousing took place gradually over the next 30 years, and it was not until the mid-1930s that the relocation was completed. During the German bombing in the 1940s the old Blackfriars premises were destroyed, but the Streatham Road works emerged virtually unscathed, proud to have sustained production throughout the war despite severe shortages of raw materials, and for many Mitcham residents Pascalls came to be regarded as one of the enduring facets of life.

James Pascall & Sons' works, c.1970

As James Pascall & Sons Ltd. approached the centenary of the company's foundation the immutabilty of the association of Pascalls with Mitcham seemed absolute. Sadly, nothing in life remains the same, and the announcement in the local press in 1959 that Pascalls had been purchased by the Beecham Group presaged the far greater shock when it became known that the group's confectionery interests were to be sold to the Cadbury-Fry organisation. Extensive reorganisation of production and marketing was almost inevitable, and by the early 1960s the fate of the Mitcham factory and its employees had been determined. The economics of what, since the abolition of rationing in the 1950s, had become an increasingly competitive industry, dictated a transfer of production to Cadbury's factories at Birmingham and Bristol. Closure of Pascalls' Mitcham factory was announced in March 1970,[6] and by May 1972 the demolition contractors were well advanced in their task of razing the Furzedown Works to the ground. Proposals for using the land for housing were rejected by the Borough Council, which wished to see the site retained for light industry, and in January 1973 the *Borough News* reported that the first units on the 'Mitcham Industrial Estate' were nearing completion.

The destruction of so prominent a landmark and, moreover, the ending of Pascalls' long association with Mitcham left many local people with what can only be described as a sense of bereavement. For those with childhood memories of Streatham Road it will be a long time before the tall brick chimney, the works' hooter – a familiar sound, audible right across north Mitcham – and the delicious smell of chocolate and boiled sweets fades from the memory.

Until house-building recommenced in the 1930s there were allotment gardens behind Pascalls works, and the writer recalls one allotment holder keeping goats on his patch. Yet more allotment gardens were to be found at the northern end of Hill Road, it having been stipulated when the Avenues Estate was first under consideration that land should be set aside for this purpose. During the 1939–45 War, and the period of food rationing that lasted until the early 1950s, these allotment gardens even supported a flourishing piggery. The houses in Hill Road largely date from the 1920s, with some later infilling. Undeveloped land did not stand idle for long in the inter-war years, and Garden

Avenue, offering slightly larger accommodation than was the norm in terrace housing, was completed soon after the Armistice. Beecholme Avenue, Elmhurst Avenue and Edgehill Road, the latter an extension of Hill Road, followed in due course, completing by 1934 the house-building as far as the Tooting and Mitcham Football Club's stadium in Sandy Lane.

Just before the 1914–18 war Gorringe Park, or Sandy Lane, School was built by the Mitcham Local Board as an elementary school, catering for infants and juniors of both sexes up to the age of 12. According to a report in the local press in November 1944, when fire damaged the roof of one department of the school, the bell fell from the wooden turret in which it had hung. On examination it was found to be inscribed "The Gift of Mrs Penelope Woodcock to the Sunday School and Parish of Mitcham 1791". No one at the time could remember how the bell came to be removed from the Sunday Schools building on Lower Green West, which had closed as a National Day School in 1897. When the writer endeavoured to trace this historic bell in 1965 the school caretaker

Gorringe Park School c.1920

disclaimed any knowledge of it, and it would appear that this link with the past was removed with the debris.

Finally, to this period of inter-war development belonged the 1930s dairy, bakery and laundry of the Royal Arsenal Co-operative Society, off the Driftway and extending through to Sandy Lane. The dairy, which received bulk supplies in road tankers, contained the latest pasteurising and bottling plant, and supplied a large area of South London daily. The bakery, opened in February 1935, was designed by the Society's architect and built and equipped by the R.A.C.S.'s Works and Engineers' Department. A two-storey structure in reinforced concrete, it boasted the latest features of hygienic design and the most modern bakery equipment then known.[7] As might be expected, both dairy and bakery were showpieces for the Co-operative movement. A similar two-storey building housed the R.A.C.S. laundry. Close to Sandy Lane there was a two-storey stable block, an unusual arrangement, to accommodate 30 or more delivery horses. The buildings on the site survived the 1939–45 war and remained in use by the R.A.C.S. until the 1980s, but were demolished in 1986 to provide a site for housing.

Group I, Gorringe Park School, c.1909

NOTES AND REFERENCES

1   THE MIDDLE AGES

The Background

1   Morris J., (Gen. Editor) *Domesday Book 3, Surrey* (1975) 6,4.

2   Mawer A. and Stenton F.M., English Place-Names Society Vol. XI *The Place Names of Surrey* (1934) 52:

 "*Swynes, Swaynes* t. Hy 7 *AddCh*, probably deriving from the family of Robert *le Sweyne*, found in Morden in 1296 *(WAM)*".

3   Ekwall E., *The Concise Oxford Dictionary of English Place Names* (1936). This latter work is, however somewhat dated, and needs to be treated with caution. See also later editions (1951) 40

4   By the mid-10th century Merton comprised an estate in the gift of the King. It was easily reached via "Stane Street", the main highway out of London to the south-west, which passed through Tooting and Colliers Wood.

5   Morris J., (Gen. Editor) *Domesday Book 3, Surrey* (1975) 8,24

 There is also an "alleged" charter dated AD727, purporting to confirm a grant of land in Mitcham by Erkenwald. *Victoria County History of Surrey* IV (1912) 230, quoting Birch, Cart. Sax. i, 64, no.39

6   Morris J., op cit 8, 25, 26

7   Burns D., *The Sheriffs of Surrey* (1992) 51

The William Figges, father and son

1   Lysons D., *Environs of London* I (1792) 351, quoting Harleian MSS. Brit. Mus. No. 313. f.20 and

 Manning O. and Bray W., *History and Antiquities of Surrey* II (1809) 496/7

2   Burns D., *The Sheriffs of Surrey* (1992) 51

3   Manning & Bray *ibid.*, 496–7

4   *Ibid.*, 497

5   *Victoria County History of Surrey IV* (1912) 233, quoting Chanc. Inq., a.q.d., file 136, no.8

6   Chanc. Inq., a.q.d., file No. 136, no.8

7   *Victoria County History of Surrey IV* (1912) 233, quoting Chan. Inq., a.q.d., File 220, No.12

8   Manning O. and Bray W., *History of Surrey* II (1809) 497

9   Heales A., *The Records of Merton Priory* (1898) 226 quoting Escheat Rolls 20 Ed II No. 39 (BM Add MSS Symms 413) and

         Victoria County History of Surrey IV (1912) 231, quoting Cal. 1226–57

10   *Victoria County History of Surrey IV* (1912) 233, quoting Chanc. Inq. p.m. 23 Edw. III, pt. ii (lst nos.), no. 15, also

         Lysons D., *Environs of London* I (1792) 351–2

         Also *Calendar of Fine Rolls VI (Edward III 1347–1356)* (1921) 123 and 124

11   *Calendar of Close Rolls X* (1908) 308/9

         The medieval Hall Place was not demolished until 1867.

12   *Victoria County History of Surrey IV* (1912) 233, quoting 35 Ed III m.3 d.v, and *Calendar of Close Rolls* Edw. III XI 302

13   *Calendar of Close Rolls* XI (1921) 244

14   Lysons D., *Environs of London I* (1792) 352, quoting

         Esch. 6 Hen. IV No.45

15   Pound Farm, an open hall house of obvious medieval date, which stood off London Road in Upper Mitcham until it was demolished in the late 19th century, is a possibility. There is no documentary evidence to support the idea, however, but there was a pound in the farm yard.

The Estate of Merton Priory in North Mitcham

1   Manning O. and Bray W., *History of Surrey* II (1809) 498, and *Victoria County History of Surrey* IV 231

2   Morris J., (Gen. Editor) *Domesday Book 3, Surrey* (1975) 5,6

3   Heales A., *The Records of Merton Priory* (1898) 84, Cart. No. 236 & 237, fo, cxviii.v

4   *Ibid.* 141, Cart. No. 332, fo. cxliii

5   Lysons D., *Environs of London* I (1792) 352, quoting Cott. MSS, Brit, Mus. Cleopatra C. vii. fol. 127 a

6   Heales A., *The Records of Merton Priory* (1898) 105, quoting Cart. No, 288 fo. cxxx

7   Beddington Inclosure Act 1819, 59 Geo. III c.11

8   Heales A., *The Records of Merton Priory* (1898) 110–111, quoting Cart. No, 278, fo. cxxiii. The property was a fee of Sir Matthew de la Mare.

9   *Victoria County History of Surrey* IV (1912) 231, Feet of Fines, Surrey, 27 Hen. III no.8

10 *Ibid.*, Feet of Fines, Surrey, 32 Hen. III no.52

11 Hopkins P., 'The Mauduit Lords of Mitcham' *Merton Historical Society Bulletin* 135 (September 2000) 12–14

12 Heales A., *The Records of Merton Priory* (1898) 91 & 97, quoting Pedes fin. 17 Hen. III. Surrey, No. 165

13 Lysons D., *Environs of London* I (1792) 351, Cotton MSS. Brit. Mus. Cleopatra, C. vii. f, 116

14 Heales A., *The Records of Merton Priory* (1898) 117, quoting Cart. No. 223, fo. cxvi. v.

15 *Ibid.*, 124–5, quoting Charter Rolls, 36 Hen. III m.11

16 *Victoria County History of Surrey* IV (1912) 231, quoting Cal. Inq. p.m. 1–9 Edw. II 346, Feudal Aids v. 124

17 Heales A., *The Records of Merton Priory* (1898) 215, quoting Eschaet Rolls, 8 Edw. II No. 68 (Brit. Mus. MSS Symm's Collection fo.11 v. and fo. 301).

    A 'knight's fee' was an area of land held by a knight (or his tenant) for which he was liable to give military service, or money in lieu, to his overlord.

18 *Victoria County History of Surrey* IV (1912) 231, quoting Pope Nich. Tax (Rec. Comm.) 206 and Heales A., *The Records of Merton Priory* (1898) 174–5 quoting *Taxation of Pope Nicholas IV* (Rec. Off. Ed.) p.208 b

19 Heales A., *The Records of Merton Priory* (1898) 249, quoting Inq. p.m. 21 Edw. III, Surrey, No. 47 (B.M. Add. MSS 6169 p.125)

20 Heales A., *The Records of Merton Priory* (1898) 287, Bodleian Library MS., Laud 723, fo. 102

21 *Victoria County History of Surrey* IV (1912) 231. See also Heales A,, *The Records of Merton Priory* (1898) App. CLII, p.cxxv, quoting 'Account of John Bowland, Collector of rents in the Manor of Byggying in Micham', Ministers' Accounts, Co. Surrey, 29–30 Henry VIII No. 115, Mem. 7

22   Heales A., *The Records of Merton Priory* (1898) 259–60, quoting Inquis. ad quod damnum, 46 Ed. III, No. 56 (Brit. Mus. Add. MS., Symm's Collections, fo, 399)

23   *Ibid.*, 291 quoting Inq. p.m. 22 Ric. II

24   Mawer A., and Stenton F.M., English Place Names Society IX. *Place Names of Surrey* (1934) 52

25   Heales A., *The Records of Merton Priory* (1898) 186–188

26   Ekwall E., *The Oxford Concise Dictionary of English Place Names* (1950) 42

27   Surrey History Centre 599/219. Translation of grant in fee-farm of the manor of Biggin and Tamworth to Robert Wilford, 1544.

28   Surrey History Centre 599/221. Translation of inquisition post mortem for Robert Wilford.

29   *Victoria County History of Surrey* IV 231 and Heales A., *The Records of Merton Priory* (1898) App. CLII p.cxxvii– cxxvlii

30   Heales A., *The Records of Merton Priory* (1898) App. CLII p. cxxv Ministers' Accounts Co. Surrey 29–30 Henry VIII, No. 115, Mem. 7

31   A portion of "Flemymede", in the tenure of Sir Thomas Hennage, was not granted to Wilford. (Surrey History Centre 599/219) It is believed this lay to the north of the Graveney, in the parish of Tooting.

2   THE MANOR OF BIGGIN AND TAMWORTH

1   Brayley, E. W., *A Topographical History of Surrey* IV (1841) 88

2   Heales A., *The Records of Merton Priory* (1898) 159–160

3   *Ibid.*, 134/5 Justice Henry Bigod presided.

4   Surrey History Centre. Court Rolls of the Manor of Biggin and Tamworth

5   Mitcham tithe survey map and register.

6   Heales, A., *The Records of Merton Priory* (1898) 215

Gilbert the ninth Earl of Clare and eighth Earl of Gloucester had been a powerful and enthusiastic supporter of Simon de Montfort, fighting with him at the battle of Lewes in 1264. The family possessed castles at Tonbridge and Bletchingly, and inherited vast estates in Surrey, Suffolk and elsewhere in the kingdom. The male line of the Clare family was finally extinguished at the battle of Bannockburn in 1314. Hearnshaw F., *Surrey, its Place in History* (1936) 73

7   Manning O. and Bray W., *History of Surrey* II (1809) 498

8   Heales, A., *The Records of Merton Priory* (1898) App, CLII cxxv Ministers' Accounts, Co, of Surrey, 29–30 Henry VIII No. 115. Mem. 7. These accounts, which are in the P.R.O., contain much detail of the estate.

9   *Victoria County History of Surrey* IV (1912) 231

10   Manning O. and Bray W., *History of Surrey* II (1809) 498, quoting Terrier in Surrey, Donation MS. Brit. Mus. 4705. Also Surrey History Centre. 599/219 a–b Copies of grant in fee-farm of the manor of Biggin and Tamworth and other lands in Mitcham, late Merton Priory, 1544.

11   Lysons, D., *Environs of London* I (1792) 352–3, quoting Pat. 36 Hen.VIII. pt. 27. May 19, and the manorial court rolls, extracts from which were supplied to him by the steward, Mr R. Barnes.

12   Surrey History Centre. 678/l. The will of Robert Wilford was proved at London 23 October 1545. Details of his estate in Mitcham and elsewhere in Surrey are given.

13   British Library. Add. MS 23561. Confirmation ('Exemplification') by Queen Elizabeth at the request of Henry Whitney, Serjeant of Thomas Bromley., Kt., Lord Chancellor 15 July 1580.

14   British Library, MS 23500. Exemplification of the accounts of Biggin and Tamworth, late held by Merton Priory, 1585

15   Surrey History Centre. 212/73/4

16   Surrey History Centre, 212/73/7

17   Surrey Record Society, *Surrey Quarter Sessions Order Books* XXXV (1934) and XXXIX (1938).

18   "Plan of Farms and Lands in Mitcham being the estate of John Manship, Lord of the Manor of Biggin and Tamworth" is dated 1743, and presumably was prepared shortly before the sale was finalised.

Transferred personally by the author from Mitcham Vestry Hall to Mitcham Library in 1965 for safe keeping. Taken from Mitcham Library to Surrey Record Office (on extended loan) *c*.1966. Now missing.

19   Other authorities, already quoted, similarly recount the descent of the manor, albeit with slight variations.

20   *Victoria County History of Surrey* IV (1912) 232

21   *Victoria County History of Surrey* IV (1912) 231

22   Lambeth Archives (Minet Library). MSS 1802: 'A Survey and Valuation of an estate call'd Merton Abbey in the parish of Merton als. Marton in the County of Surrey.' 63/719 S,505. S.R.

23   Canterbury Cathedral Archives MSS 70,436. John Middleton's Survey of Vauxhall Manor Waste Land 1806.

24   Montague, E. N., *A History of Mitcham Common* (2001)

25   Merton Local Studies Centre. Typescript copy of Evidence of Henry Tanner in Ecclesiastical Commissioners v. Bridger, 1890. Also in Surrey History Centre 320/3/1/12

26   Croydon Local Studies Library & Archive Service. Harold Williams Collection of Sale Particulars, Part 3 Outside Croydon. S 243 – 'Particulars, Conditions of Sale, and Plan of the Remaining Portion of the Valuable Estate of the Late James Moore Esq.' 29 August 1853. Lot 81

27   British Library Map Room; Maps 137 c.6. Manor of Biggin and Tamworth and properties offered for sale, 1888,

28   *Victoria County History of Surrey* IV (1912) 232

3   FIGGES MARSH

1   The Main Ditch was shown on the Borough Engineer's surface water sewer plan, consulted in 1965, commencing as two contributory streams, one from the junction of South Lodge Avenue with Galpins Road, and the other from Yorkshire Road, meeting in the vicinity of the then Pollard Oak public house (subsequently renamed the Oak and Acorn and demolished 2001 to make way for housing). From here the Main Ditch flows beneath Fern Avenue and the rear accessway between Greenwood and Vale Roads. Beyond Manor Road it crosses the cemetery grounds and the former Pain's Firework factory site (now the Eastfields Estate), the culvert thus far measuring 6 feet by 3 feet in section. From the end of Acacia Road, skirting the south of Lonesome primary school, it was shown on the plan as 7 feet by 3 feet. It crosses Grove Road and runs under the entrance to Firs Close. After crossing the railway where one original bridge wall is still visible, it passes under Edgehill Road and Mitcham Industrial Estate before reaching Streatham Road. Here it turns briefly south-west, and then, opposite Sandy Lane, turns again to follow Manship Road to the commencement of Figges Marsh. Beneath the footpath across Figges Marsh it flows to Carlingford Gardens, and then

turns left under Gorringe Park Avenue, and right beneath the London Road until it discharges into the Graveney opposite Tooting Station.

2   Reporting the felling in March 1973, the *Merton Borough News* stated that 2,000 elms had been lost in the Borough to Dutch elm disease. Depressions in the grass alongside the path across the Marsh still show where several of the trees stood.

3   The area between the footpath and Manship Road, now part of Figges Marsh, appears from late 19th century maps to have then been enclosed land.

4   *Merton Borough News* June 1973

5   The idea was not taken up in view of the obvious maintenance implications.

6   The distinctive pattern of strip fields (albeit with signs of some amalgamation) can be seen in the Mitcham tithe map of 1847

7   See, for instance, the map of Surrey produced by C. & R. Greenwood dated 1st. September 1823

8   Surrey History Centre (formerly Guildford Muniment Room). Book of Sale Particulars G/85/2/1 (2) No.12

9   Surrey History Centre. 320/1/3

10   Daniel Lysons, in 1792, wrote "A small common in this parish went by the name of Figg's-marsh, now usually called Pig's-marsh."

     "Pig's Marsh" was the term used in the O.S. map of 1816, and this was copied by A. Bryant (1823) and the Greenwoods. It was still in use by map makers in 1862, when Edward Stanford published his *London and its Suburbs*. "Figg(e)s Marsh", however, continued as the "official" name and was used in the vestry minutes, the Post Office *Directory of the Six Home Counties* published in 1845, the tithe commutation surveyors, and by Crawters, when they prepared a plan for the auction of the late James Moore's estate in 1853.

11   Mitcham Vestry Minutes

12   Canterbury Cathedral Archives MSS 70,436 (Transcribed by Roy Edwards of the Streatham Society in 1983)

13   Surrey History Centre. Plans of Land in the manor of Biggin and Tamworth 2/6/5–8

     Customary Courts Baron held by Thomas I. Penfold, following the death of James Moore, 25 January 1855, 2 March 1855 and 2 June 1855

14   Merton Local Studies Centre. Particulars of the Sale by Auction of the Estate of the late James Moore in 1853. Lot 53 comprised a "Homestead consisting of Stable, barn, Yard, Piggeries, cottage (including dairy), and house, occupied by John Henry Bunce (leased to the late W. Harland)".

15   Slater B, "Memories of Mitcham" in Bidder H.F., (Gen Editor) *Old Mitcham* Part I (1923) 24

It was not unusual for cows from Swains Farm to be seen on Figges Marsh in the 1920s. (Mrs Audrey Thomas in a personal communication)

4   TOOTING JUNCTION TO LAVENDER AVENUE

Road and Rail

1   Edwards J., *Companion from London to Brighthelmston* Pt. 2 (1801) 16

He describes the Graveney as a small "rill".

2   28 George II c 57

3   A map in Surrey History Centre, K/2/6/6, shows the position of the toll house.

4   "An Old Resident" (E. Bartley), *Mitcham in Days Gone By* (1909) 8

5   Merton Local Studies Centre. Tom Francis Scrapbook. George Sheppard (b.1855) recalling his boyhood in an undated article entitled "The Coloured Past", cut from *Mitcham Advertiser*

5   Drewett J.D., "Memories of Mitcham" in Bidder H. F. (Gen. Editor) *Old Mitcham* II (1926) 5

6   The names of three of the toll collectors are known from the census returns:

George White   (1841)

William Busby   (1851)

Richard Williams   (1861)

In early days the toll-gate keepers were sworn in as parish constables, and empowered to detain felons within the toll-house.

Tooting Old Hall

1   *The Queen's London,* Cassell (1896) 163

2   *Sutton Advertiser* 31 May 1879

3   Walford E., *Greater London* (1884)

4   *Dictionary of National Biography* XIX 280

5   Morden W.E., *History of Tooting-Graveney* (1897)

6   Tithe map reference 50: "Workhouse Meadow" (at junction of Swains Lane and London Road) and

     map reference 49: "Workhouse Garden" adjoining, to the north.

7   Surrey History Centre. Plans of land in the manor of Biggin and Tamworth, K/2/6/7 and K/2/6/8

8   Surrey History Centre CC 28/121

     The Local Government Board Provisional Order Confirmation (No. 16) Act 1903

Swains Farm

1   Morris J. (Gen Edit.) *Domesday Book 3. Surrey* (1975)

2   Mawer A. and Stenton F. M., English Place-Names Society Vol. XI *The Place-Names of Surrey* (1954) 52

3   Merton Local Studies Centre. Particulars of the Sale by Auction of the Estate of the late James Moore in 1853

Figges Marsh, or Tamworth, Farm

1   Greenwood C. & J., *Surrey Described* (1823) 104

2   Notably in Rocque's map *The Environs of London* 1741–5, and map produced in Edwards' *Guide* of 1789.

3   Drewett J.D., "Memories of Mitcham" in *Old Mitcham* II Gen. Editor Bidder H.F., (1926) 10

4   "An Old Resident" (E. Bartley), *Mitcham in Days Gone By* (1909) 8

5   Surrey History Centre 413/8/19 & 20

6   Surrey History Centre. Copy Plan of the Estate of Mrs Waldo, (Late Peter Waldo). 2553/13

7   Surrey History Centre. Mitcham Land Tax records.

8   Surrey History Centre. Plans of Estates in the manor of Ravensbury

9   Post Office Directory 1845: "Holland and Barber, farmers, Figges Marsh",

         Mitcham Tithe Commutation Register 1846: "The Executors of William Holland, and Isaac Barber"

10   Census 1861

11   Surrey History Centre. Plans of Land in the Manor of Biggin and Tamworth K/2/6/5–8

         Customary Courts Baron held by Thomas E. Penfold, following the death of James Moore, 25 January 1855, 2 March 1855 and 2 June 1855

12   *Mitcham Mercury* Charter Day Souvenir September 23 1934 15

         The Mitcham seat, which had been won by the Conservative Party the previous year in a straight fight with the Liberals, was relinquished by Sir Cato Worsfold of Hall Place, Mitcham, and provided a safe seat for Sir A.S.T. Griffith-Boscawen, the Minister of Health, who had lost Taunton at the general election. In the 1923 by-election a rival Conservative 'queered the pitch' and as a result of the split vote, James Chuter Ede, ex-teacher and secretary of the Surrey Association for Teachers, won the seat narrowly for Labour. Nine months later, Richard Meller regained the seat for the Conservatives.

         Robinson D., 'Surrey Elections and M.P.s from the Reform Act to the Present Day' *Surrey History* Vol. 5 No. 5, 288

London Road Cemetery and Tamworth Farm Recreation Ground

1   Of Temple Court, Wray Park Road, Reigate. (A 1920's Reigate *Directory*)

2   Col. Stephen Chart, Town Clerk of Mitcham, in a lecture given to Mitcham Civic Society, *c.*1946, and the *Official Guide to Mitcham* of the 1930s.

3   Bailey A.H., 'The Commons and The Greens', *Mitcham Mercury* Charter Day Souvenir 21 September 1934, 16

4   *Merton Borough News* December 1966

5   *Merton Borough News* March 1973

6   Information from Parks Department, London Borough of Merton, December 1997

The Poplars

1   Edwards J., *Companion from London to Brighthelmston* Pt. II 16

2   Merton Local Studies Centre. Mitcham Local Illustrations Collection, and Montague E. (Edit.) *Old Mitcham* (1993) plate 28

3   Surrey History Centre. Mitcham vestry minutes.

4   Montague E.N., *Mitcham Workhouse* (1972)

5   Surrey History Centre. Mitcham land tax records, and poor rate books

6   Surrey History Centre. Mitcham land tax records, and

      Pigot & Co.'s *Directory* 1826–7, which has the entry:

      "Burns, Rev. – (curate)" under "Nobility, Gentry and Clergy".

7   Surrey History Centre. Plan of the Estate of Mrs Waldo in 1805. 2553/13

8   *Post Office Directory* 1845: "John England Rudd Esq." recorded at "the Poplars"

9   Mitcham tithe map and register reference 77

10   Bartley E., "Rural Mitcham" in Bidder H. J. (Gen. Edit.) *Old Mitcham* II (1926) 33

11   *Dictionary of National Biography* LIX 15

12   Ellis H., *My Life* (1940) 73–9

13   Merton Local Studies Centre. Tom Francis, in notes to Miss Farewell Jones dated 1st. July 1932.

5   POTTER AND MOORE, "PHYSICK" GARDENERS OF MITCHAM

1   *Pharmaceutical Journal and Transactions X* (1850–51) 115

2   Slater B., "Memories of Mitcham" in Bidder H. F. (Gen. Edit.) *Old Mitcham* I (1923) 24

3   Malcolm J., *Compendium of Modern Husbandry* III (1805) 116

4   *The Gentleman's Journal and Gentlewoman's Court Review* 16 May 1908

5   Heales A., *The Records of Merton Priory* (1898) 187–188

6   Bradley R., *Botanicum, a Botanical Dictionary for the Use of the Curious in Husbandry and Gardening* (1728)

7   Potter & Moore, *Recorded History of the House of Potter and Moore, distillers of Lavender at Mitcham, Surrey, since 1749* (Undated booklet, early 20th century).

8   Lysons D., *Environs of London* I (1796) 350

9   Surrey History Centre 413/8/19 & 20

10   Edwards J., *Companion from London to Brighthelmston* (1789) Pt. II 16

11   Mitcham vestry minutes.

12   *Victoria County History of Surrey* IV (1912) 232, quoting

       Com. Pleas D. Enr. East. 44 Geo. III, m.58

13   Merton Local Studies Centre. Mitcham Illustrations Collection.

14   Surrey History Centre. The Court Rolls of the Manor of Biggin and Tamworth under the lordship of James Moore are in four volumes, K/2/1/14–17 inc.

15   Greenwood C. & J., *Surrey Described* (1823) 186

16   Merton Local Studies Centre. Tom Francis Collection of Slides. Also reproduced in Montague E., *Mitcham. A Pictorial History* (1991) Plate 39

17   Surrey History Centre. Plan of Estates of Mrs Waldo in 1805. 2553/13

18   Public Record Office Death Duty Register I.R.26 – 1905 folio 213/5 shows these two ladies to have been James Moore's natural daughters by different mothers. The 1851 Post Office Directory gives her address as " 'Clock House', Upper Mitcham." Jemima Scriven later became Mrs de Boudry.

19   Chart R.M., "Mitcham Parish Church" in Bidder H. F. (Gen. Editor) *Old Mitcham* I (1923) 9 and

       Worsfold, C.T., *Memories of Our Village* (1932) 10

20   Surrey History Centre. LA/5/8/3–30. Certificate signed by Captain Thomas C. Thompson at Battle Barracks on 3rd. June 1799.

21   Public Record Office. W.O. 13 4060. Pay lists and other documents to 1813

22   Walter Hunt (born c.1850), addressing Mitcham Adult School, *c.*1933. News cutting in Tom Francis's scrapbook, Merton Local Studies Centre. Ben Marchant seems likely to have been the male child born to Elizabeth Marchant on the 24 July 1817, of which James Moore was cited as the

father in a Certificate of Bastardy sworn before William H. Merle J.P. of Colliers Wood on 6 October 1817. Ben Marchant later became the landlord of the "Horse and Groom" in Manor Road.

23   Mitcham Tithe Map and Register.

24   Public Record Office. Death Duty Register I.R. 26 – 1905 folio 213/5 (transcribed by the late Jack Bailey of Merton Historical Society) and *Victoria County History of Surrey* IV (1912) 232

25   Merton Local Studies Centre. Sale Particulars.

26   "James Bridger lived at the Manor House from 1858–1885, when he died." (James Bridger junr., giving evidence in Mitcham Common Conservators v. Ecclesiastical Commissioners 1909) Mitcham Local Collection – transcript of proceedings.

27   Census 1841

28   Drewett J., "Memories of Mitcham" in Bidder H. F. (Gen. Edit.) *Old Mitcham* II (1926) 4–5

29   Walford E., *Greater London* II (1898) 525

30   *Victoria County History of Surrey* IV (1912) 232

31   "Mr James Bridger's daughter Gertrude E. Bridger, married Mr Frederick Armfield of 'The Chestnuts' ". She died in 1946, aged 82.

      Merton Local Studies Centre. Tom Francis's Scrapbook. Newscutting dated December 1946

32   Merton Local Studies Centre. LP414 L2 (668.5) 1953

      Information from Mr F. H. Priest of W. J. Bush Ltd.

33   *The Gentleman's Journal and Gentlewoman's Court Review* 16 May 1908

6   RENSHAW'S CORNER

The Oxtoby Houses, or The Chestnuts

1   Anthony Quiney, G.L.C. Historic Buildings Division, in pers. comm. 1969.

2   One of the Oxtobys' apprentices in the 1780s was John Chart, son of the parish clerk, whose firm, Chart and Sons, was appointed in 1819 to rebuild Mitcham parish church. Merton Local Studies Centre. Mitcham Local Collection: Mss notes by Miss Farewell Jones.

3   Surrey History Centre. Copy will of Samuel Oxtoby of Mitcham,
         Carpenter, dated September 1761, proved PCC by Roseman his widow
         29 January 1768. 413/8/11

4   Manning O. and Bray W., *History of Surrey* II (1809) 503

         The money was payable from an estate in Mitcham, and the bread was
         to be distributed at the church every Sunday morning by the
         churchwardens.

5   Mitcham tithe register

6   Census 1841

7   Merton Local Studies Centre. Tom Francis scrapbook. News cutting
         dated December 1946. Gertrude Armfield died in 1946 aged 82.

8   Information from the occupier of No. 1 in 1972.

9   Local Post Office directories

10   Drewett J.D., 'Memories of Mitcham' in Bidder H. F. (Gen. Edit.), *Old
         Mitcham* II (1926) 9

11   E.g., the Post Office directory 1851

12   Croydon Libraries, Norbury Local Studies Collection: Harold Williams
         collection ref. No. 309. Sale particulars of "The Chestnuts", Figges
         Marsh, Upper Mitcham, dated 25 June 1896.

13   Montague E.N., 'James Pain & Sons, Firework Manufacturers' in *Surrey
         History* Vol. IV No.1 (1989/90) 35–

14   Renshaw, John F., & Co. Ltd., *Marzipan* (1950)

Lock's Lane and Eastfields Road

1   Drewett J.D., 'Memories of Mitcham' in Bidder H. F. (Gen. Edit.), *Old
         Mitcham* II (1926) 9 & 10

2   Merton Local Studies Centre. Plan produced by Blake and Carpenter
         for the sale on 9 May 1898

3   John F. Renshaw & Co. Ltd. 'Marzipan' (1950), and Hirst A., 'It's Nuts
         to all Bakers for Your Festive Delight' in *Merton Borough News*
         November 9th. 1979

4   *Merton Borough News* July 1990

5   Surrey History Centre CC 28/11. Lock's Lane to Greyhound Lane.
         Inquiry re repair, 1896–1897.

The Willows and Manor Cottage

1   Drewett J.D., 'Memories of Mitcham' in Bidder H. F. (Gen. Edit.), *Old Mitcham* (1923) 10

2   Census 1861

3   Green's *South London Directory* (1869) 124

4   Tithe register and map

     A clue to the early history of part of the site may lie in a copy of the court rolls of the manor of Biggin and Tamworth, recording the surrender in May 1854 by Josiah Lucas and the admission of James Childs to land originally enclosed by Oxtoby with the consent of the manor. Surrey History Centre. 173/4/2

5   Census 1851

6   *Environs of London* 1741–5

7   Kelly's *Directory* 1882

8   British Library Map Room 137c 4 (15)

9   It is still shown on the 1899 edition of the 25-inch O.S. map

10   Smith C. & J. "Surrey"

7   BIGGIN FARM AND GORRINGE PARK

The Tudor and Stewart Periods

1   Surrey History Centre.

2   Ordnance Survey Geological Map

3   *Victoria County History of Surrey* IV (1912) 231,

     quoting Pat. 36 Hen. VIII pt. xxvii

4   Rice R.G., 'On the Parish Registers of SS. Peter and Paul, Mitcham' in *The Reliquary and Quarterly Review* 142 note 29

5   British Library. Add. Ms. 23559 Will of John Pyke of Bygginge, yeoman

6   Surrey Record Society *Abstracts of Surrey Feet of Fines 1509–1558* XIX 80 etc.

7   *Surrey Archaeological Collections* IV (1869) 72

8   British Library. Add. Ms. 23558

9   London County Council *Court Minutes of the Surrey and Kent Sewer Commission 1569–79* (1909) 237, 251

Flemingmeade was included amongst the demesne lands of Merton priory, and is mentioned in the Ministers' Accounts of 1538. In 1600 it was granted (with other lands) to Nicholas Zouche, and thereafter until 1607 passed through various hands. P.R.O. /C/66 etc.

10   'Lay Subsidy Assessments 1593/4' in *Surrey Archaeological Collections* XIX (1906) 41

11   British Library. Add Ms. 23563

12   Surrey History Centre. 212/73/6

13   Surrey History Centre. 599/360

14   The fields listed in 1650 were:

Biggin ffurzes	17½ acres
Tidmire Meade	17½ acres
Tidmire Coppice	10 acres
Grainly Close	
Long Ffurlong	15½ acres
Barne Close	4 acres
adjoining parcel	2 acres
Tidmire Hill	7 acres
Busshie feilde	20 acres
Wheate close)	
Little close)	20 acres
Homes Meade	2 acres
Ilande meade	2 acres

15   Surrey History Centre. 212/73/7

16   Surrey History Centre. 212/73/16

17   Surrey Record Society, *Surrey Hearth Tax* Nos. XLI, XLII, Vol. XVII (1940)

The 18th Century

18   Transferred personally by the author from Mitcham Vestry Hall to Mitcham Library in 1965 for safe keeping. Taken from Mitcham Library to Surrey Record Office (on extended loan) *c.*1966. Now missing.

19   Surrey History Centre. Book of Sale Particulars. G85/2/1 (2) No. 12

20   Surrey History Centre. James Cranmer's Estate Memorandum and Estate Book.

21 Manning O. and Bray W., *History of Surrey* II (1809) 498

22 Surrey History Centre. 599/290

23 Jowett E., *Morden Park, Morden* (1977) 1 and 7

24 Surrey History Centre. Mitcham poor rate books.

25 The somewhat unusual surname suggests that Edward Evanson may have been related to the Revd John Evanson, vicar of Mitcham from 1734 to 1778.

26 Surrey History Centre. Land tax records.

An indenture of 1794 (Lambeth Archives (Minet Library) 3384) describes John Manship as of "Lamb's Conduit Street, Middlesex".

27 Edwards J., *Companion from London to Brighthelmston* Part II (1789) 16

28 Hughson J., *London* V (1808) 338

Biggin Grove and the Matthews

29 Kenrick N.C.E., *The Story of the Wiltshire Regiment* (1963) Appendix I, 231

30 Dr Robert J. M. V. Howard, then Registrar in Psychiatry at the Maudsley Hospital, in a pers. comm. *c.*1990.

31 See also Allderidge P., *Bethlem Hospital 1247–1997* (1997)

Lord Redesdale and Tamworth House

32 *Dictionary of National Biography* XIII (1921–2) 527/9

33 Merton Library Service. Extra Illustrated copy of Brayley E.W., *History of Surrey* III

34 Surrey History Centre. Book of Sale Particulars. G85/2/1 (2) No. 12. Sale Particulars, Tamworth House, March 1818

35 Greenwood C. & R., *Surrey Described* (1823) 275

36 Surrey History Centre. Book of Sale Particulars. G85/2/1 (2) No. 29

Gorringe Park House and William and Fanny Harris

37 Surrey History Centre. Collection of Deeds relating to Mitcham. 570/

38 Pigot and Co.'s *Directory* for 1826/7 lists "Fuller, Wm. Esq., Biggin" under "Nobility, Gentry and Clergy."

39 Mitcham Tithe Commutation Register and map

Farmhouse, garden, rick yard, plantation, farmyard and buildings have the reference numbers 10–13

40   McGuffie T.H., 'Kelly of Waterloo' in *Army Historical Research* Vol 33 (195– ?) 97–109.

Kelly (1774–1828) died at Mullye in Nepal, having attained the rank of Lt.-Col. and the position of Deputy Adjutant-General to the British Forces in India.

41   Wilson D., vicar of Mitcham, *Pastoral Letters*

Gorringe Park – The Last Years

42   Kelly's *Directories* e.g., 1903

It was still described as his seat in the *Victoria County History of Surrey* IV (1912) 229

43   According to local residents, Gorringe Park House was not used as an orphanage until after Lipshytz left.

44   Francis T., on page 97 of his lantern slide notes (kept by Merton Local Studies Centre) states that Mrs de Boudry's sister, Charlotte Matilda Cooper became a Mrs Owen, and that it was her son who, after inheriting the De Boudry Chapel (the former "Major's Chancel") in Mitcham parish church, sought to sell it.

Work by the late Jack Bailey of Merton Historical Society and the Society of Genealogists showed that Charlotte Matilda Cooper (1809–1877), daughter of James Moore, married Thomas Owen (1793–1862) of Welshpool at Mitcham in 1829. There were four children of the marriage; Frederick, Henry M. (b.1831), Matilda Anne (b.1836), and Emily (b.1843). At the time of the Census in 1851 Charlotte and Henry were staying at the Manor House, Mitcham, with her half-sister Jemima Scriven (1809–1886) who in December 1851 married the Revd Daniel de Boudry. Henry was described as being "in the Wine Trade". It would appear that it was he who had inherited the De Boudry Chapel.

Although it has not been established with certainty, Henry's son seems likely to have been Joseph Owen (1881–1943), who lived at Pentlands, St George's Road, Mitcham, and was managing director of the Tamworth Park Construction Company, one of several firms of building construction and estate developers active in Mitcham in the 1920s and '30s. The land on which Mitcham Library now stands was presented by him to the Urban District Council, and during the building he also gave much of his time as clerk of works. His public spirit and generosity were recorded in a plaque still to be seen above the door leading to the former reference library. It was unveiled by his wife at the official opening in May 1933.

Joseph Owen was chairman of the Mitcham division of the Liberal Association, founded the North Mitcham Improvement Association, and was chairman of the Urban District Council in 1923.

Mitcham Mercury Charter Day Souvenir 21st September 1934, 15

45   Hurley G., "Ratepayers Hall Built at Cost Price" *The Gazette* August 31st. 1972 10.

This is an excellent resumé of the history of the early days of the North Mitcham Improvement Association, and the emergence of the Borough of Mitcham.

46   *Merton Borough News* April 1978

8   STREATHAM ROAD

Roe Bridge

1   Quoted by Hobson J.M., *The Book of the Wandle* (1924) 96

2   Hughes, A., 'The Manor of Tooting Bec and its Reputed Priory' in *Surrey Archaeological Collections* LIX (1962) 6

3   He was, for instance, instrumental in securing the enclosure of part of Moorfields for use as a burial ground for the poor of London.

Brown J.W., *Roe Bridge, Mitcham Lane* (1993)

4   Graham Gower, of the Streatham Society, in a personal communication. quoting (with a note of caution since the writing on the 17th century document is difficult to decipher) London Metropolitan Archives M 95/BEC/22/29.

5   Brown J.W. *Roe Bridge, Mitcham Lane* (1993)

A Country Lane

1   Hughes A., 'The Manor of Tooting Bec and its Reputed Priory' in *Surrey Archaeological Collections* LIX (1962) 6

2   Brown J.W. *Roe Bridge, Mitcham Lane* (1993)

3   Malcolm J., *A Compendium of Modern Husbandry* III (1805) 311

4   Bartley E., 'Rural Mitcham' in Bidder H.F. (Gen. Edit.) *Old Mitcham* II (1926) 34

5   Drewett J.D., 'Memories of Mitcham' in Bidder H.F. (Gen. Edit.) *Old Mitcham* II (1926) 3

6   Merton Local Studies Centre. Tom Francis Lecture Notes. Sir Cato
        Worsfold, in his *Memories of Our Village* (1932) retold the story, with
        embellishment.

Urbanisation

1   Nairn I, and Pevsner N., *The Buildings of England. Surrey* (1971) 370

2   Merton Local Studies Centre. Pastoral Letters of Canon D. Wilson.

3   Hurley G., 'The Vicar Who Came to Build' in *The Gazette* October 25
        1972 10

        The Revd Baker's reminiscences were published in *The Gazette* in 1939

4   Surrey History Centre. 2327/1 Sale Particulars of Manor Farm

5   *1866–1966 Pascall ... one hundred years* (1966)

6   *Merton Borough News* March 1970

7   *A Review of a Modern Bakery opened by the Royal Arsenal Co-operative
        Society Ltd. at Mitcham* (Undated, *c.*1935)

Shops in Streatham Road, c.1911

INDEX